50a

THE FASHION HOUSE

INSIDE THE HOMES OF LEADING DESIGNERS

LISA LOVATT-SMITH

conran
OCTOPUS

This book is for Nicolas and Sabrina
who have to put up with living with
a frantic, emotional, overworked writer
rather than the perfect muse and
mother they deserve.

First published in 1997 by
Conran Octopus Limited
37 Shelton Street
London WC2H 9HN

ISBN 1 85029 898 X

Commissioning Editor: Denny Hemming
Senior Editor: Jenna Jarman
Editorial Assistant: Helen Woodhall
Copy Editor: Sarah Sears

Art Editor: Alison Barclay

Picture Research: Clare Limpus

Production: Julia Golding

British Library Cataloguing-in-Publication Data
A catalogue record for this book is available from
the British Library

Printed and bound in China

CONTENTS

FOREWORD

When this book was proposed to me, warning bells rang. Anyone with an iota of common sense should have realized that doing a book that featured twenty of the world's foremost fashion designers would be logistically almost impossible. The eminent among them design between four and six collections a year, and sometimes oversee more than twenty. This hectic routine is known as the fashion circus, and with good reason. The cloistered, panicked 'absolutely not available for interviews' of before their shows is immediately succeeded by an absence, as the designers jet off to some exotic location to recover from their seasonal ordeal. Before the next catwalk these luminaries of the fashion world have to find the time actually to live in the houses illustrated in this book, as well as furnish them and entertain in them. And the fact that some of them have acquired five or six homes makes this lifestyle even more unwieldy, despite the obvious advantages the designers enjoy – private jets, helicopters and endless staff.

After ten years of watching fashion collections, season after relentless season, however, I did know exactly how passionate certain designers were about their homes. A few years ago Gianni Versace gave me an insight into his fascination with interiors when, despite being surrounded by deferential press at a crowded cocktail party, he jumped up enthusiastically and whispered, 'Come with me, you must see my bedroom.' Undaunted, I followed him upstairs, where he delightedly showed me the perfect painting to go with his neo-classical bed. I had never seen him quite so excited about a frock.

This book features a selection of houses which range from a humble pad in a high-rise to a palatial thirty-room mansion. They are all much-loved, carefully thought-out homes. Yves Saint Laurent has woven a strangely obsessive tale around Proust's A la recherche du temps perdu into the very structure of his Normandy retreat, a haunting exercise in abstraction and beauty. Eric Bergère confesses that he would have been a decorator if he hadn't happened to have a seamstress grandmother, and his apartment is a dialogue between his favourite neo-gothic theme and his enthusiasm for South American religious fervour: a rich and lush combination of gold tablecloths and raspberry-red walls.

I have always been fascinated by the concept of the creative 'whole', the entire artist. Perhaps I am irrevocably condemned to a lifetime of frivolous thought, but I have only ever warmed to painters and sculptors who, like Brancusi or Duncan Grant, Picasso or Man Ray, lived in a world that intimately reflected their art. I have never perceived creativity as a day job, nor can I relate to artists who live their lives distanced from their production. For me, the most tender and revealing facet of an artist is his or her approach to what we often belittle by calling the decorative arts:

the quirky, anecdotal, perhaps even self-indulgent, element – Beaton's scribbles in the margins of his letters, Colette's recipes, Dali's museum, Bérard's jewellery designs, Monet's garden, Cocteau's pottery. It may all be peripheral art but it is so enlightening in its spontaneity. My fascination for the early twentieth-century 'enclaves' of like-minded creative people of many different disciplines – the Bauhaus, Bloomsbury, the Ballets Russes, even the interior design practice of Jean-Michel Frank – stems from this appreciation of different elements of visual life being unified by one prevalent aesthetic. The homes of fashion designers reflect this perfectly, despite Pierre Bergé's naughty, teasing comment: 'The link between fashion and interiors? ... At Yves Saint Laurent, unlike certain other Houses, we are not in the habit of making dresses that look like sofas.'

Fashion is the most decorative of the minor arts: it involves the same delicate balance of structure, textiles and accessories as the decorating profession itself. More interestingly, as increasingly we adopt those 'feminine values' so vaunted by the media, this readjustment in the balance of power between the sexes has produced a gentler world, where decorators and dressmakers who pander to that sensibility have themselves become an integral part of society's party set; no longer mere purveyors of services to an elite, they are regarded rather as the powerful catalysts who can realize the dreams of the majority.

Tellingly, when I asked the designers what they would change about their homes if they could, most of them answered, 'nothing'; after all, these are professionals of proportions, connoisseurs of colour. When I told Bill Blass about the proposed book, his deliciously rich voice boomed back at me over the transatlantic airwaves: 'Fashion designers' houses are the best,' adding mischievously, 'Some designers would have made better decorators, don't you think?'

Lisa Lovatt-Smith

AZZEDINE ALAIA

Azzedine Alaia is practically the only Parisian designer of stature to have remained independent. His view of women fundamentally altered fashion design in the 1980s, and he has spawned a thousand imitators. He remains unclassifiable. He has the following of a fashion guru, the attitude of a tailor and his finished products are often pure couture. He has never adhered to the *chambre syndicale*, the governing body of Paris fashion, and yet his success has been extraordinary and his clients are almost religiously faithful. His is a unique set-up within the fashion world.

Alaia has always lived among women, and there is a warm, gossipy, homey, reassuring and sometimes delightfully malicious atmosphere to his home and workroom. Other designers are confounded by the fact that the world's most elusive models have a uniquely close relationship with him, but the reason is quite simply that going to visit Alaia is, in many respects, like going home to your mother: if the girls are not looking after themselves, he scolds them; he gives them advice on their love life; makes up a bed for them; and feeds them quantities of couscous. Alaia marries Arab hospitality to the down-to-earth qualities that he has inherited from his grandmother – by all accounts a forceful woman and a major influence – and then applies the combination lavishly.

Alaia's intimate relationship with women began when he was a child, while he played unqualified assistant to Madame Pineau, the French midwife who had delivered him. Between one birth and another Alaia studied her collection of fashion magazines and Madame Pineau encouraged his curiosity. The idea he had then of Paris as the promised land – high heels and lipstick, belted, curvy 1940s elegance that

Opening pages: Perforated leather corsets from the 1992 summer collection, three of them displayed on a glass cabinet in Alaia's home. Left: A view of the period mural on the first floor of the *verrière*. Above: Wabo, one of Alaia's six dogs, seated on a nineteenth-century wooden omnibus bench.

exemplified a world of chic and substance – influenced his aesthetic for life. He soon learned to sew, and, by pretending to the local seamstress that his fine stitches were his sister's, he paid for his paints and books at art college by sewing.

Two Tunisian sisters with influence in Paris took him under their wing. They procured a *stage* for him at Dior. But it was not the five-day stint there that revealed his vocation; rather, it was the two subsequent seasons that he was to spend at Guy Laroche. The couture ateliers of 1959 initiated him into fashion at the highest level, and two years as a baby-sitter for the Comtesse de Blégiers were to prove the finishing touch to his education. She introduced him to her aristocratic friends, women who had been brought up to dress in couture, who understood the faultlessness of the couture ideal, and who were to refine the young Arab boy's natural perfectionism. The poet Louise de Vilmorin was to introduce him to Greta Garbo and Arletty, and a further handful of blue-blooded ladies who were to become his first, formative clients.

In 1982 an article in Italian *Vogue* revealed that Claudia Cardinale and Paloma Picasso were abandoning the ornate ormolu salons of the conventional couturiers to be measured up for skintight patent leather numbers by a tiny Tunisian, who worked out of three rooms in the rue de Bellechasse. This was at a time when other designers, influenced by Comme des Garçons and Yohji Yamamoto, were tending towards voluminous 'shrouds'. Undeterred, Alaia continued to uplift the bust, whittle the waist, dissimulate the *derrière* and generally, in the words of Lauren Hutton, 'make sex clothes'.

Far left: A Julian Schnabel canvas behind a glass mannequin wearing a knitted Alaia dress, embroidered with sequins. Left: A 1930s Burghalter chair and ritual Dogon masks from Africa. Above: The broad staircase and the disused elevator shaft on the first floor.

Nowadays he has moved his whole operation to a disused warehouse in the Marais. The shop is on the ground floor, with the designer's studio directly above it and his private apartment on the top floor. 'At first I visited some *hôtels particuliers* – the kind of structure one immediately thinks of as being suitable for a fashion house. But then I realized that all that was too sumptuous for me. I didn't feel at ease. So I began to look for something industrial, something that would not be overbearingly impregnated with the feeling of the past. I like luxury with a poor spirit to it. It is important that when someone walks in, they don't feel oppressed. Here you can sit down just anywhere, whether your pants are clean or dirty, and you don't have to worry. It had been a department store warehouse, workshops and even a cheap working man's canteen; the menu is still painted up on the wall, complete with prices. So it had the right feel for me. It felt like a place that one could work in. There are good vibrations, I think, because there has only ever been work here. Its past and its present is full of work. And the dogs live here, whereas if I'd bought an eighteenth-century palace, well, it wouldn't have been such fun.'

Alaia's six irrepressible dogs come in assorted sizes, colours and tempers. They rule the roost to the palpable discontent of a pair of haughty Persian cats, who live upstairs in the bedroom. 'The atelier is small dog territory, and the big dogs are kept under the *verrière*.'

Far left: Part of Alaia's collection of vintage fashion photography. He is a pioneer in this domain as fashion photography has only recently begun to be considered collectable at the same level as reportage photography or fine art. These images are mostly Irving Penn shots of the 1950s icon Bettina Graziani, a friend and fan of Alaia.

Left: A view of the 'glass cube' dining room where Alaia usually serves lunch. The room was built specially, above the shop and just off the *verrière*. The glass furniture is by Sabino, and dates from the 1920s. The paintings are by Condo and von Weyhe.

Above: A close-up of the Sabino radiator screens. The photographs are again by Penn.

'I like luxury with a
poor spirit to it.'

The *verrière* is a perfectly proportioned, glass-ceilinged hall with an iron balcony. It occupies half of the entire structure. 'It was all subdivided but I could see the potential underneath ... It was perfect for my shows: simple and not heavily decorated. I directed the work myself for two years, clearing everything away and revealing the structure. I really enjoyed doing that. Then I brought in an architect because I did not know anything about electricity, water supply or foundations.'

Above: Several bolero jackets with intricate embroidery: 'work in progress' in the design studio by Alaia's cutting table, where he spends most of his time. The pell-mell on the column includes family snapshots and photographs of female icons, such as Arletty and Tina Turner.

The key to understanding Alaia's way of life is a proper appreciation of the fact that in an Arabic home the rooms are largely non-specific. To the Western world this is a very new concept; to Alaia it just means that you chat, work and sleep when and where the mood takes you. Indeed, Alaia the workaholic is often found curled up fast asleep on his cutting table. It hardly seems worth climbing up the stairs to his mattress on the floor, even if it is surrounded by designer furniture and paintings. In this imposing building there are no barriers between home and shop, office and workshop, friends and employees. The Islamic concept of the extended family reaches out and welcomes you in, as long as you are not too pretentious.

It was contemporary painter Julian Schnabel – now a close friend – who transformed Alaia's home into a magnificent artwork. The shop downstairs is a masterful mix of deep purple paintings, African sculpture, 1940s furniture and Schnabel clothes racks. Upstairs he combined huge canvases in gilt frames, dramatic red curtains, wood and plaster; he gave a sense of proportion, a *grandeur*, to the project.

Above: A view of the fitting room, with a photograph by Peter Lindbergh and paintings by von Weyhe. The chairs, part of Alaia's extensive collection of furniture, were salvaged from a theatre.

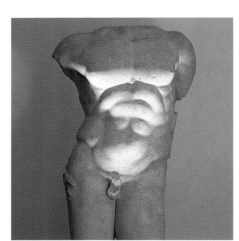

GIORGIO ARMANI

Giorgio Armani is one of the five most powerful fashion designers in the world. The index that tells us this sort of thing procures its figures from such realities as net profits, net exports and other dry details; it does not, of course, tell the whole story. In purely fashion terms Armani is powerful because, as recently as the late 1970s, he changed the way a certain type of women dressed – for ever. He is probably one of the only living designers about whom you can say that; his clothes defined an age.

In 1975 he sold his Volkswagen and set up his own company. After eight years designing for a ready-to-wear men's tailoring company in Milan he knew nearly everything there was to know about making jackets. So he made jackets. He made them soft, he made them light, he made them to live in, and, most importantly, he made them for women. Now, any busy woman will confirm that the easiest answer to professional wear is a trouser suit, and Coco Chanel would be the first to tell you that it should *look* elegant but *feel* comfortable. Foreseeing this need, Armani restructured the jacket entirely. He played down the shoulder pads, took out the lining, moved the buttons and enlarged the armholes. Urban professionals, young and old, Italian, American – even French – women loved the way he had taken the stiffness out of the suit. In men's fabric, but with loose trousers and long jackets that skimmed the body, in subtle neutral colours, his suits were not subject to fashion's swings and roundabouts. An Armani suit was a fashion investment. With none of the overt trappings of wealth, it whispered rather than shouted power.

Opening pages: A torso and, with its simple lines and pale furniture, a corner of the living room. Left: The entrance hall, graphically punctured by dark window and door surrounds. Above: On display in the hall: a model of a 1940s car, a Man Ray picture, a Chinese box and a little terracotta sculpture.

The key to the designer's influence lies in the fact that women did not buy just one Armani suit; they bought lots, hooked on the comfort and the ease of it all. In 1981, anticipating an increasing interest in cheaper lines, Armani launched Emporio, and appeared on the cover of *Time* (the first designer to do so since Dior). Ten years later he launched the A/X sportswear concept in America, and his designs were monopolizing Hollywood parties, with stars in thrall to his style. But even with all this transatlantic activity, Milan-based Armani was still living in this apartment – 'over the shop', as he puts it.

'Until a few months ago the building also housed part of the Armani office and people would just drop in on me. Now I've finally shut the door: the office has been moved down the street. I absolutely never design at home. My home is my home and my work is shut out, forbidden! This is a refuge for my body and my spirit; something that is mine alone and which does not belong to Armani the public person.' This public Armani is in great demand, and is overworked. He is known to be incredibly focused, and with the weight of the million-dollar business entirely on his shoulders – and he owns 100 per cent of the company,

Above left: The large living room has been arranged to give the impression of intimacy; like the rest of the house, it is furnished entirely with Jean-Michel Frank pieces, which Armani calls 'icons in wood, parchment and fabric'.

Centre: A Jean-Michel Frank writing table and screen in what Armani calls his 'thinking room', where he spends most of his time when he is at home, valuing the peaceful atmosphere. Also boasting a fireplace, it is perfect for relaxing or letter-writing.

Left: A detail of the writing desk which is the focal point of the quiet little study.

which is a unique situation in the fashion business – he needs to be. It must be lonely at the top, but unlike some of his colleagues, Armani does not feel the need to be seen to frequent the social arena; he prefers the company of an intimate group of friends whom he has known for a very long time. And he has dinner with his mother at least twice a week – she is 88 years old and, as he says, 'her simplicity and her strength have influenced my whole life.' His sister Rosanna is also one of his closest associates.

'I am at home only early in the morning when I exercise, have breakfast and read the papers ... sometimes I get an hour's break for lunch ... and I have the evening ... if I'm not out. My favourite room is the study, where I chat, relax, watch television and curl up in front of a roaring fire. In my home, as in my work, I have no time for trivialities that are totally useless even at an aesthetic level. My designer's eye refuses unrealistic shapes, vulgarity in a fabric, or in colour. I have chosen to make both my home and my fashions restful and gently natural. The similarity between them lies in the seductive choice of materials ordered by what I like to call a lyrical geometry. This is the true luxury of simplicity – I love the "invisible" element of true elegance. I hate things that are immediately obvious and inharmonious. I suggested to Peter Marino, the architect who has also designed some of my boutiques, that the reference point should be a period of the past that in my opinion went perfectly with the structure of the building. That suggested Paris in the 1930s, epitomized by the furniture of Jean-Michel Frank with its great simplicity of lines, love of neutral materials, modernity without futurism.'

Right: The leather-walled dining room described by Armani as 'spacious and with particularly well-thought-out lighting – important when dining with ladies'. The rectangular table is made of oak, and the chairs of sycamore.

'This is the true luxury of simplicity – I love

the "invisible" element of true elegance.'

One could apply that criteria to Armani's clothes also, because they transcend fashion, much as his interior design transcends decoration. It is a study in simplicity, and as mannish as his signature suits. One feels that the process of elimination, whether applied to his fashion design or to his home, is an essential driving force. Asceticism or luxury? There are no rich fabrics here, no strong colours, no apparent eccentricity, but there is extravagance of a sort: the extravagance of living so simply when one could possess so much. It is not minimalist exactly; rather it is a space that is totally controlled.

His four homes in Milan, Saint-Tropez, Lombardy and Pantelleria (a tiny Mediterranean island between Tunisia and Naples) are one of his passions. 'I love to restore interiors. I have lots of homes, all completely different from one another but all somehow "Armani". When I buy a house my primary concern is that it must fit seamlessly into the environment, while at the same time expressing my own personality and taste. I have no idea whether my homes are the way they are because I am a fashion designer, or whether I am a fashion designer because I have the gift of taste which is expressed in my homes.'

Above left: The comfortable proportions and harmonious tones of the bedroom. The wood-panelled walls add to the monastic effect. Above right: An equally unfussy jacket from the collection. Right: The bathroom, with a light-diffusing wall, and with Armani's favourite soaps and colognes on show.

GEOFFREY BEENE

In an impressive silver-and-white book on Geoffrey Beene published in 1995, there is a curious title to his biographical notes. It reads 'A Chronology of Flight', and the most moving entry is for 1946 when the designer was just 19 years old and studying medicine in New Orleans, in the American Deep South, where he was born. It reads: 'Confronts cadavers. Abandons Medicine. Flees the South for Los Angeles. Forgoes University of Southern California. Works in the display department of I. Magnin.' What New York's contemporary gurus in psychology would make of the accumulation of negatives and the fascination with flight is worthy of speculation. Such a paragraph could only have been written by Beene himself, or very much under his influence, because, strangely, he prides himself on his reputation as perverse.

Beene was one of America's first fashion revolutionaries and iconoclasts. Beneath the old-fashioned Southern charm and the impeccable manners of a perfectly brought up Louisiana princeling, who grew up in a world not that far removed from Scarlett O'Hara's, lies a passion for radical fashion. Despite having dressed more than his quota of society queens, he has done it according to his own vision. Since the early 1970s he has often abandoned structured garments in favour of a free-flowing, soft silhouette, light and easy to wear. He removes padding and structuring, zippers, buttons and fasteners. A confirmed nonconformist, he eschews that career-woman staple: the suit. One of his celebrated one-liners runs: 'Dressing for success is something unsuccessful women do.' He has imposed his reputation for streamlining the female anatomy, and invented a style that never, ever, hinders a woman in her movements, or indeed in her choice of lifestyle. More often than not Beene cuts on the bias, with invisible

Opening pages: A view of the red lacquer living room, and a satin shoe from the collection in Beene's favoured print – first conceived for the house.
Left: Portraits of the designer's dachshunds and a pair of fringed silk gloves. The armchair has been upholstered in yellow-and-white fashion fabric.

seams slithering flatteringly around the body. He sculpts the shapes of women with this liquid geometry based on cut and it has earned him the label of modernist. A doyen of Seventh Avenue, the heart of the New York fashion world, he abandoned it for new headquarters in 1989, having paved the way for a new generation of American fashion minimalists. Since then he has celebrated 30 years in fashion and become a 'runway runaway', preferring to present his clothes on dancers, on a stage. One of Beene's all-time classics was the sequinned floor-length soccer shirt of 1968, meant to be worn to a ball; another of his innovations was introducing flannel, denim and tweed to the gala circuit. All this qualifies him as an agitator, although you would never guess so from his kindly, courtly ways.

His Oyster Bay retreat on Long Island's north shore, where he spends his weekends, is a similar kind of visual contradiction. From its serene, plain neo-Palladian exterior it is impossible to guess that inside lie rooms as rare as treasure chests: pink and red walls, animal prints on the floor and furniture, hundreds of orchids and bowls of sensuous vegetables in place of more conventional flower arrangements.

Previous pages: An overall view of the living room stuffed with treasures from Beene's extensive travels. Above: The dining-room walls were painted by Jack Plaia to evoke the fur of a snow leopard's belly. The centrally placed carpet continues the animal-skin theme.

Left: The stool is Indian but it has been covered in the ubiquitous black-and-white spotted print. The satin jacket is by Beene, inspired by the interplay and balance of the design on the dining-room walls.

'I was attracted by the Palladian architecture, and the perfect proportions. It had the added advantage of being close to New York, and on the water. The house is rather like an estate on the French pattern,

but in miniature. What I was really looking for was a home for all the antiques I have collected over the past 35 years. As far as the colours, fabrics and furniture are concerned, fashion is always there.' The pace of the fashion world is there too, in the pace at which Beene changes the decoration, always in search of the new. It has been French provincial, grand and muted in turn. 'Initially I was seeking to evoke a richness but I quickly tired of that, so I changed things. Like my clothes, this house evokes a combination of the humble with the rich.' In fact, one gets the feeling that this fashion maverick would be moving house and not just changing the decor, were it not for his family's reproaches about his inability to settle down!

The dining room is particularly striking: Beene had the walls painted to evoke a snow leopard's spots. Inspired by a French schoolchild's notebook, and characterized by the abstract and graphic elements that Beene adores, the pattern has almost become a Beene signature, making its way onto shoes and gloves – even appearing on the walls of his new boutique. It was a lucky inspiration but, as Beene remarks, there is a trial-and-error aspect in decorating that is similar to building up a fashion collection. Overflowing with sublime animal prints, the overall effect of the room is so perfect that it hardly seems possible that Beene did not employ a decorator. 'Being a designer makes the whole decorating process easier,' he points out: the blue upholstery in his papaya-coloured bedroom reworks a colour combination that he has used in fashion; and he describes his red living room as he would fabric: 'Red is a neutral; colour flows with it.'

This hands-on attitude is typical of the man. He works all morning by himself in the neighbouring orchid greenhouse, which he had built specially to house his collection of over 2,000 different plants. His treasured exotic blooms inspire him too. 'I have often wanted to express the sensuality of the orchid in my clothes but I don't know if I've quite managed it.'

'My fashion is liquid geometry.'

Far left: A dress from the collection, expressing the architecture and geometry that evoke the house. This is a common occurrence in Beene's world – the interplay between his visual universes is constant.

Left: A guest bedroom, with the bed set in a sleeping alcove lined with nineteenth-century trompe-l'oeil panels.

Below: A close-up of Beene's geometry and its original inspiration in the foreground.

ERIC BERGERE

Eric Bergère has an amusing theory to explain the apparent discrepancy between the distinctive modernity of his fashion designs and the flamboyant glamour of his colourful Paris apartment. It all stems, he maintains with a mischievous twinkle, from the startling disparity between his two grandmothers.

'One is very strict, and always austerely dressed in beige cashmere twinsets, grey flannel skirts and flat shoes. She is tall and slim with great *allure*, wears big camelhair travelling coats belted at the waist, and nearly no make-up. She is an adorable grandmother but most of all she is the epitome of chic, good taste and distinction, and represents the masculine–feminine fashion ideal. My other grandmother is peroxide blond, plump and cuddly, and utterly sweet, and paints her very long nails a different colour every day. She is a dressmaker and still passionate about it at 87 – she's a great one for saving things and makes incredibly kitsch patchworks out of leftovers. Even the tiniest bit of material that I give her is transformed into something inconceivable: a dress made out of 28 different prints, for example. She is very spontaneous, and very creative, and although she seems to combine colour and material haphazardly, there is an intuitive symmetry to her work. Her taste shines through the mess. It is quite fascinating. Of course it was she who taught me dressmaking; sewing was the only way that she could keep us kids busy and I was the one who got hooked. They are completely different women and very inspiring in two completely contradictory ways. I find that I am always as attracted by the most absolute minimalist chic as by the baroque, accumulative, colourful side of things. This flat is my Mae West side getting the upper hand over my Katharine Hepburn side.'

Opening pages: The rich decor is enhanced by cushions in Lacroix couture fabric and velvet by Sabina Faye-Braxton. Left: An eighteenth-century Italian lamp in gilded wood next to a nineteenth-century armchair and footstool in a Faye-Braxton velvet. Above: A velvet stole by Bergère for Lanvin.

One of Bergère's most persistent themes, which is equally apparent in the clothing he designs, is a passion for everything medieval and neo-gothic. Perhaps this stems from having been born in the thirteenth-century city of Troyes. 'It is quite an incredible town – much like Paris must have been before the great fires and town planning. There are seven flamboyantly Gothic churches in the centre of town, and on my way to piano lessons, I used to walk down alleys where the houses leaned over so much that they touched each other overhead. All these images are engraved in my memory.'

This taste for Gothic and ecclesiastical objects and architecture was obvious even at the age of 19, when he was plucked straight from fashion school to design womenswear for Hermès. The appointment of such a young man caused a tremendous stir, but Bergère surpassed expectations and surprised everyone by producing very grown-up collections. With his respect for the perfect cut, he slotted naturally into a fashion house that had a tradition of classical elegance, its roots in the world of made-to-measure uniforms, riding clothes, 'proper' tailoring and all the dignity and strictness that an approach such as that entails. 'The tunic, the monk's habit – the simple forms that I love are all refined, dignified, pure and yet comfortable. They enhance the body. Clothes must not be worn to be shown but to give the wearer a

Opposite left: The gracious neo-Napoleon III sofa in the bedroom has been upholstered in contrasting velvets bought in Egypt. The curtain tie is a 'gothic' chain-mail belt that was originally draped around a model's waist for a show.

Opposite right: The neo-Louis XVI sofa has been painted black for elegance; the cushions are from Syria. The fireside chair is upholstered in cheap and cheerful synthetic fabric picked up in the souk in Tangiers.

Left: Two Eric Bergère printed silk scarves entwined beneath an antique embroidered cushion, bought on a trip to Jaipur.

certain *allure*, a look.' The aesthetic match worked so well that Bergère ended up staying at Hermès for nine years. 'I was young, and I felt free. I could do what I liked and I liked everything that I was doing. It left its mark on me and for a long time afterwards whatever I did workwise seemed a bit flat.'

Bergère went on to design for Erreuno, taking over from Giorgio Armani. Several years of moonlighting followed before he felt ready to start his own label. 'A commercial piece of clothing has a standard collar, a standard sleeve, a standard build ... which is why everybody ends up making the same things. I had my head full of: "Eric, this is not wearable, long sleeves will trail in the soup." I felt strongly the constraints of 15 years of commercial design.' He was feeling frustrated. 'Because I was working for other people, I had lost the detachment – I felt that I no longer knew what I liked and disliked. I felt uninspired, unable to express myself. So I poured all my energy into decorating this flat.'

The sprawling nineteenth-century building, in pure Napoleon III style, seduced him with its poetry; he was initially attracted by its 'faded *grandeur*'. It is very nineteenth century, but done with the memory of eighteenth-century proportions. It dates from a time when architects, reflecting the taste of the established

Above: A view of the library with its imposing inlaid chest from Syria. The portrait is a 1930s copy of a Renaissance painting of a conquistador. The clock on the mantelpiece was a present from Bergère's seamstress grandmother, who first encouraged him to become a fashion designer.

'This flat is my Mae West side getting the upper hand over my Katharine Hepburn side.'

power, appreciated Romanticism and favoured a return to historical periods like the Middle Ages or the Baroque – a time of operetta nostalgia, flamboyant and decorative. 'I couldn't help loving it. It was filthy, the carpet was soggy, bills were piled up by the door, but the flat had soul.'

Today the apartment is most remarkable for the very distinct atmosphere evoked by each of the large and well-proportioned rooms. 'I treated the apartment just like my very own first collection. I set about it exactly as if I was preparing a catwalk show. It had one major advantage over a collection: there I would have been able to explore only a few themes, whereas with the apartment I was able to create a very different palette and mood for every single room. The study is very gothic and was painted with English paints in turquoise and chocolate; the library is all red and very *latino*; the blue bathroom is cooler and more French. It was like developing a fashion theme: the materials, the colour ranges, the accessories ... To my mind, fashion and decoration are very strongly linked. A piece of clothing is a matter of proportion:

Above left: Portuguese plates on an Indian cotton tablecloth. The coloured glasses are Spanish, the cutlery Scandinavian. The candlestick is from a church. Above right: The dining room, with three portraits by Layla d'Angelo – one of Bergère as a matador. The large painting is by Philippe Pasqua.

the collar has to be proportional to the buttons, to the pocket ... the lining fabric has to work with the buttons and the detailing ... It is exactly the same exercise as staging a room. You come into the empty room and have to put a piece of furniture where its proportions will sit well, corresponding to the right colour, to the right material. It's all about balancing the constraints and having an eye for things. Sometimes I try out colour combinations on the walls that have worked in garments or vice versa.'

Bergère uses huge amounts of fashion fabric – for upholstery and curtains. He explains that with new colour collections appearing every six months, this offers much more choice than upholstery fabric. 'I use couture fabrics without hesitation, including all sorts of remnants for cushions and things.' Indeed, there is the odd armchair upholstered in fabric otherwise used for a $15,000 evening dress.

It is undoubtedly Bergère's extensive collection of religious icons, however, that forms the most important focus for the apartment. Most of them have been brought back from travels in South America, where he was 'very impressed by the decorative and joyful aspect of Catholicism ... The Indians, Mexicans and Peruvians interpret religion their way and have for centuries, which gives it a naive and popular note. In these countries where gold and silver have always been abundant and glorified, the grand aspect of religion gives a bizarre expression to worship. Some religious images become nearly pagan – images of wealth almost. To Western eyes that is a complete contradiction, but to them it is natural.'

Bergère surveys the colourful jumble of baroque images around him, the blood-red library walls and the quantities of textiles and objects. 'I did once consider becoming an interior decorator rather than a fashion designer. In fact, my ideal of decoration would be a pure white convent or monastic cell. But perhaps', he smiles laconically, 'I'm not *quite* ready for that yet.'

Far left: An English Victorian mahogany chest of drawers dominates the navy blue bedroom, which leads in to the pale blue bathroom. A flamboyant, embroidered bedcover from Istanbul graces the neo-gothic bed.

Left: The bathroom, with a neo-Louis XVI sofa in the foreground. The velvet cushions, bought in a Cairo market, and the rug and throw, in alpaca fur from Peru, all add to the glamorous atmosphere.

BILL BLASS

Bill Blass refers to himself as 'the old boy', acknowledging the fact that not many survive at the top in the fickle world of fashion, where you first have to make the ladies look good, and then, as the years roll on, make them look even better. Blass has been one of the top names on Seventh Avenue and has been dressing an exclusive circle of the richest and most powerful women in the world since the 1950s. His clients are New York society's 'ladies who lunch', who wouldn't actually dream of eating but who push extortionately priced food around on their plates instead, before going on for fittings. For decades they were the lifeblood of French haute couture. It was when World War II immobilized life in France that Blass and a few other home-grown talents surfaced, and fashion history changed course. Americans began to have their own style, and Blass, with his 'hands-on' trunk shows and his pioneering sportswear licence, was a key player; he had been sketching glorious evening gowns and impeccably cut suits 'as good as any in Europe' since the early 1940s, and was well qualified to assist at the difficult birth of a true American fashion industry which had stood in awe of Paris for so long. Inspired then by the great theatrical costumiers, his approach has remained all but the same, and his clothes have never lost their glamour.

A major Bill Blass gown is a classic; carefully thought out and impeccably constructed. Visual impact and quality are his trademarks. His home can be described in the same way, for he lives in a perfectly proportioned apartment in Sutton Place, at the top of a 1930s building, which is 'one of the three great apartment buildings in New York'. Sutton Place is probably Manhattan's grandest address, but Bill Blass,

Opening pages: A detail of a Bill Blass dress and two Regency day beds in the drawing room. Left: The hall with an onyx urn from Pavlovsk Palace. Above left and right: In the drawing room: the library table is nineteenth century, the plaster medallions and globes eighteenth century – all Italian.

with his rich voice and his charming manner, is himself a very solid sort of man with a taste to match it. 'I have always thought that fashion designers are the best interior decorators,' he says gaily. 'I love it. It's all a question of the eye; you are soliciting the same innate talent.'

The apartment itself is a vision in white and dark wood, flooded with light and arranged with an irreproachable sense of style that exudes a rare serenity – perhaps comparable to wearing a Blass gown to an imposing New York society function and knowing with absolute certainty that you are dressed impeccably. 'There is a sense of dignity, a simplicity and a classicism in my clothes which can be read into the apartment. As I am surrounded with colours and fabric all day I look forward to a monochromatic home. I work in fashion – I don't want to live somewhere that looks fashionable.'

The space is made visually arresting by neo-classical features, such as fluted columns – installed by Blass – and carefully chosen Empire furniture. 'I moved in solely because of the height of the ceilings and the size of the rooms, and because they were square. I mean, square is the perfect shape for a room. Everything looks just right here. The building had such great bones: in the same way that you can't dress a woman if the bones are all wrong, it's difficult to decorate an apartment with poor structure.'

Above left: The bookcase in the bedroom-cum-library with three Greek bronze helmets; a bronze by Sir Frederick Leighton stands on an eighteenth-century Swedish desk. Above right: The bathroom. Right: An Edwardian table with a model of the Place Vendôme monument to Napoleon.

'I work in fashion – I don't want to live

somewhere that looks fashionable.'

Blass, who believes in 'editing' his home as a designer edits his or her sketches before preparing a collection, has recently put away 35 of his paintings and old master drawings, leaving the neo-classical furniture even more prominent against the plain white walls. Much of it was bought from antique shops on Pimlico Road in London. 'What I have here is the result of a lifetime of collecting. There is no relationship between the things themselves – except that I like them. You know how American women choose how to wear a dress and invest it with their own spirit: I admire that sort of philosophy, and when I collect things, I choose how they are going to look in my life. The way I decorated here was to surround myself with the things I love ... and they all have great dignity. And although I chose all the furniture and pictures, I did, as a bachelor, seek out a woman to put it all together ... I had the advice of Chessy Rayner.'

And although Blass spends most of his time at his country home, where he keeps his beloved dogs and enjoys the quiet of the country, he says there is nothing about his Manhattan home – with its view from the bed of the Hudson River and its fittingly grand entrance hall – that he would change.

Left and above: In the elegantly proportioned dining room the German chairs are upholstered in early nineteenth-century toile. The trompe-l'oeil painting is seventeenth-century Flemish.

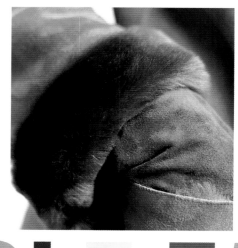

NICOLE FARHI

Nicole Farhi's singular success story has taken an entirely unpredictable course. She was born in Nice, the daughter of Jewish parents who fled from Turkey to France in the early 1920s to escape the persecution of Atatürk. Educated at the local *lycée*, Farhi was always fascinated by design. She was also keen from an early age to escape the small world of the French Riviera and to move to Paris as soon as she could, but her father was opposed to her leaving home.

At 18, with her mother's help, she managed to move to the capital, just in time to enjoy the heady atmosphere of the student rebellions of 1968. She enrolled at the distinguished Ecole Berçot and was delighted to find herself under the none-too-protective wing of an eccentric teacher who encouraged her to go out and see films, watch people, stroll; or otherwise to sketch freely. Thus, she laughs, she 'never acquired a proper technical background.' The student protests deprived Farhi of any further schooling, but by then she was already selling her sketches – at 50 francs a design – to the *bureaux de style* of the large department stores, and doing well. It is a period that she remembers with delight. 'Paris is kind to 18-year-olds; there is no other city like it,' she muses. Her daughter Candice is now living in the same apartment that her mother once inhabited – complete with mother's bashed-up old VW Beetle.

Farhi took a job designing for Pierre d'Alby, the hot young fashion entrepreneur who had spotted the budding talent of Thierry Mugler and Jean-Paul Gaultier. In 1973 he introduced her to his London agent, the dashing and volatile Stephen Marks – the beginning of a romantic and business partnership. Together, despite hot-headed moments when Farhi would cry over the patterns or fly back to Paris from London

Opening pages: A suede jacket with fur cuff from the winter 1997 Farhi collection and an antique Louis Vuitton monogrammed trunk. Left: A view of the entrance hall with the black-and-white stone flags that the designer loved immediately.

'I am mostly influenced by

without warning, they built up French Connection, and using fabric imported from the East, and often manufacturing there too, they brought exotic post-hippy chic to British consumers with instant success. By 1985, ten years after Candice was born, the company was floated on the stock market.

In 1983 Farhi launched her own company, to provide women with the casual elegance and the muted palette that they could make part of their everyday lives. The question of ease is crucial to her; she will swing her arms around to demonstrate how important it is that armholes are cut big enough, and she

Above left: The model of Farhi's wedding ring, made for her when she married David Hare. It was designed for her by Emma Paolozzi, daughter of her friend and mentor, the sculptor Eduardo Paolozzi. Above centre: The drawing room, with its coffee table made from two carved Indian doors.

my work as a sculptor.'

stresses comfort and practicality above all. Farhi has become a British fashion classic and heads that even rarer thing: the British fashion empire. Amicably separated from Marks, but still his working partner, Nicole lives with her husband, playwright David Hare, in a large, handsome house in Hampstead, north-west London. It was the graphic impact of 'the square marble flagstones in the hall' that first attracted her in 1980. The house is an uncanny reflection of her fashion: 'comfortable and easy-going'. And, as in her clothes, the influences have been eclectic. 'I furnished the house while I was travelling to the Far East to

Above right: In the drawing room the disused fireplace is now used as impromptu bookshelves. The painting above them is by Jean Gibson and the sculptures on the glass-topped coffee table in the foreground are by Eduardo Paolozzi.

design and manufacture the collections. But I stopped buying a few years ago because I did not want it to become cluttered. I also have a lot of things from flea markets, but I am mostly influenced by my work as a sculptor and the work of my artist friends.' Farhi's sculpting is her passion and she usually takes Wednesdays off in order to indulge in her art. A few years ago she bumped into Sir Eduardo Paolozzi at the Royal College of Art's foundry and the two have since become close friends – the house is dotted with plaster casts by Paolozzi as well as her own pieces.

Apart from the studio, her favourite room houses an authentic French bar. When the bar in Les Halles where she used to have breakfast was threatened with destruction she bought it outright, complete with baguette holes, coffee machine and zinc counter. 'It tends to provide the focus for a great deal of entertaining – mainly lots of people for dinner.' Their crowd makes the household one of the most enviable dinner dates in London, though Farhi's entertaining style remains relaxed: she barely bothers with a tablecloth. She has a French woman's respect and admiration for food, however, and despite her runaway runway success, declares that one of her ambitions is to be a great cook. What she really values in her home is its complete calm and the fact that it 'grew spontaneously' – as unconstrained as her designs.

Above left: The flower-filled veranda, which is original to the house, with 1930s wicker benches on either side of the plain rustic dining table.
Above right: A suit from the designer's Autumn-Winter 1996 collection. Right: Farhi's studio, where she spends as much time as she can.

ROMEO GIGLI

Romeo Gigli first came to prominence during the 1980s when the shoulderpad brigade reigned supreme. His clothes were the discerning alternative to power dressing, and thus immediately attracted a clan of fashion editors and film stars who remain faithful to him today. In his unusually quiet way he transformed the silhouette of the times. His signature outfit is still a fitted, slightly round-shouldered jacket over straight cigarette pants with cuffs – often embellished by some wondrously fragile touch in gauze, lace or beading. His palette is bewitching too, with all the colours of nature subtly merged: rust, terracotta, sage, chartreuse, eggshell. It all seemed a world away from the sharply cut monochromatic look that was prevalent then. Indeed, it still is. 'The woman I design for is feminine, and irresistibly sensual,' he declares, and with his Shakespearean name and his stubble, the man is fairly irresistible himself.

Gigli cannot simply be categorized as a romantic Italian designer, however. His poetic creations are rich in ethnic allusions; thick with the spirit of southern India, Morocco, darkest Africa or the East. During his candlelit shows, where the models may well take a leisurely stroll along a catwalk of kilims, the references to the wider world are multiple and well researched. Gigli is global in so far as he has a well-documented intellectual and visual fascination for those cultures where beadwork, lace-making, embroidery and weaving are still time-honoured arts. His low-key catwalk shows are highbrow in the sense that he weaves a transcultural fairy tale into each collection. This love for civilizations and crafts,

Opening pages: A detail of the beading on a Romeo Gigli outfit opposite a mural by Kris Ruhs behind giant burning candles standing in pebbles.
Above: Moroccan leather poufs in a room full of design classics. Right: A 1968 Swedish harp chair by Jorge Hovelskov.

'... a happy co-existence between

which, ironically, have tended to be classified as 'primitive', has encouraged him to travel and explore. His spectacular apartment in Milan is stuffed with the treasures he has brought back from his wanderings. 'I travelled for ten years before I settled down to designing. I had trained as an architect and did not turn to fashion until I was 28. Even then I had the feeling that it was essential to see and appreciate the world before trying to create things on my own.'

His apartment is in a 1920s building, a rationalist space, which is big by Milan standards. It is situated near the Trade Fair, a quiet, outlying district 'which still has oases of greenery, and while very close to the

Above left: Tribal art brought back from many trips, including enormous Papuan painted shields. Above right: The living room is furnished with classic design pieces from the 1960s, a carpet from Turkestan and a pre-Columbian tapestry on the wall behind the pillars.

things of totally disparate origins.'

centre of the city, is neither choked up with traffic nor noisy. I was looking for an island, or, if you prefer, a vast raft sailing through the clouds, from which I could pick up every patch of light that Milan's miserly skies occasionally grant us. Light is for me of the greatest importance because I measure life and creativity by the sun. That's why my home is bathed in light and all its furnishings, which are brightly coloured, are objects that play with the light, that convey buoyancy, depth and irony.'

He gutted the apartment so that he could display his pieces in a striking manner against the all-white walls. They, rather than paint or plaster effects, comprise the decoration. 'The space had the advantage

Above centre: Candlesticks from the Middle Atlas mountains in Morocco contrast with one by English pottery designer Clarice Cliff.
Above right: The unframed plain wooden door is flanked by two primitive wooden artefacts.

of being malleable. The way it was built enabled me to disembowel it and re-model it.' Thus, the apartment is simply a backdrop for the extraordinary objects that he has accumulated. 'The objects relate to space in many different ways. I do not allow them to dictate my freedom of movement, or, worse still, to affect my aesthetic perception of the space itself. All too often we give in to objects and pieces of furniture because they are useful or functional. Cupboards, cabinets, caskets, lamps, tables, chests of drawers (big and small) obviously all serve a purpose, but one must be on one's guard. Furnishings tend to end up by taking over a house, by giving it a look, a soul all of their own. I have never liked homes "done" in a specific style, even with the finest furniture. They suffocate my imagination and give me the impression of living on a pre-packaged film set. So more often than not, I design my furniture myself, and do the interiors of my shops.

'I love the atmosphere in this apartment. It can still be warm and cosy even though it is immensely spacious. Everything revolves around the fire as it does in a tribal village in Africa.'

The layout is original. Gigli designed the cast-iron fireplace that dominates the long open-plan lounge area which looks as if it has come straight out of a large American country house in the spirit of Frank Lloyd Wright. The library and the dining room open straight off the lounge, and are separated by the beautiful *hammam*-style bathroom, with its giant square bath decorated by a Moroccan craftsman who was flown all the way from Marrakech to mosaic it authentically. Only the bedroom and the kitchen, with its classic Memphis-designed square table and old-fashioned kitchen range, are behind closed doors.

'I only have things in my home that I really want to live with. They are not necessarily interrelated: Indian textiles that have inspired a cape in a collection, African masks and classic design, like the Arne Jacobsen chairs, can all work together. Sometimes I do buy something in a faraway bazaar and get back to discover – horrors – that it doesn't work, but then I give it away. I don't call this process decoration.

Left: Romeo Gigli's book-lined atelier and studio, where he designs his collections. The chair is by Tom Dixon. Above: Three Oriental statuettes; the single figure on the right was brought back by the designer from his travels in the Far East.

I have simply accumulated chosen objects. Either they enable me to re-live the emotion I felt when I discovered them, or they evoke my innermost reaction to a particular place. Objects do this better than photographs, because they themselves have had to be discovered.

'I do not consider myself a collector, however. The very idea of collecting implies that something has been lost for good and depersonalized. The mind of even the most sophisticated of collectors is rational, somewhat cold. The collector is a cataloguer of reality: I want to create reality, not "freeze" it. In my home,

Papuan shields, Indian chests, Moroccan cushions, Japanese lamps and benches, South African Resistance Art, old Chinese statuettes, Scandinavian, Californian and Italian design, things by Greek artisans and lots of other bits besides – all live happily side by side. Together – they and I – we have created an atmosphere in transition, something original, that cannot be reproduced. What strikes people here is a happy co-existence between things of totally disparate origins.'

Gigli designs at home, with various aides appearing and disappearing on schedule. His time is precious: as well as his main collection, he shows in Paris, and designs menswear and a more accessible women's line. 'Home and fashion work constantly cross over. I believe that there are various "elective affinities" between the clothes I design, the spaces I design and my home. Any difference there may be arises when one takes liberties, experimenting with one's own creative ability. One must be adventurous

Far left: The mosaic bathroom, designed by Gigli and tiled by a Moroccan artisan.

Centre: A detail of draping on a Romeo Gigli dress.

Left: The bedroom, with a lamp by Noguchi. Gigli designed the bookcase on the left himself.

and want, more than anything else, to discover all of oneself. I harbour a real cult of everything that is beautiful, of everything that embraces the best of the past and present – from all over the world – and projects it into the future.

'When I emerge from the darkened seafaring atmosphere of my bedroom – decorated with sailing ships, fishing smacks and cutters – I make my way in a semi-trance towards the space (it's not really a room) that contains the enormous mosaic table where I have breakfast. This is the crucial moment, because it's when the day and I make up our minds whether we are going to agree or not; whether there is any sunshine or not; whether the endless list of things to be done will allow us any freedom or not.

'If I really have to work, then I scatter rolls of material, fabrics of all colours, paper and pencils all over the wooden floor – all through the house. I may well stay there, sitting on the ground, until the evening, with music playing at full volume. I have to feel completely free, so I put on a very old pair of tracksuit bottoms and a T-shirt; I even have bare feet. I eat very little during the day and by the evening I am tired out and starving. If my home were not my accomplice, I think everything would be much harder and more tedious. As it is, it creates exactly the right atmosphere to stimulate my creativity ... one does not design an island, a whole island, in order to be unhappy.'

Left and above: Two views of the kitchen with its industrial fittings, a mirror mosaic pillar and a set of stacking Arne Jacobsen chairs with a Memphis table by George Sowden. The lampshade is by Fornasetti.

JOSEPH

Londoners know the power of the 'Joseph touch': it was palpable in the streets of Chelsea during the 1980s as one small boutique mushroomed and became five, and magazines and conversations became littered with his logo. At the peak of the fashion consumer craze, 'Joseph' became the way to say 'chic' in English. Famously anti-mode, the English rose finally discovered her fashion sense in Joseph's matt black selection, in his nubbly knits and in his careful choice of Continental labels by the best of the truly trendy.

As a designer, retailer and instigator of the fashion moment, Joseph knows all about the concept of design affecting all areas of life. He still goes to all his London shops personally, twice a day, in the morning after his daily swim, and in the evening just before closing. He tweaks, and chats, and notes what has sold and what has not. It is this 'hands-on' attitude that makes him a masterful retailer. 'I don't want to distance myself,' he says. 'Everything I've ever learned in my life has come from talking to people.'

He obviously does some subliminal listening too, because he is always at the absolute edge of fashion, tapping into the spirit of the age with pinpoint precision. In the 1980s he succeeded in making designer dressing accessible to London shoppers. It was natural that in the more cocooning 1990s he should then launch Pour la maison for the 'nesters' and open Joe's restaurant for the 'foodies'. His approach remains unchanged, however, and he always applies the same overall view, pursuing excellent design that will characterize every area of his life. The aesthetics of fashion and interior design – both at home and work – naturally cross over to the point that Joseph uses the same designer – Christian Liaigre – for his own home and for some of his shops.

Opening pages: A picture of Celia by David Hockney, and the staircase and ebony arch in the living room, designed by Liaigre. Right: Liaigre's minimalist furniture in heavy, rich woods – made to measure to complement the harmonious proportions of Joseph's 1930s house in Chelsea, London.

Right: The dining room, where all the furniture, including the light fittings, were specially designed for Joseph by Christian Liaigre. The chairs are the neo-colonial 'Joe', named for the master of the house and now part of Liaigre's collection. The candlesticks, by Mark Brazier Jones, were acquired following an exhibition of his work in one of Joseph's shops.

Below: The view from the living room looking into the dining room. The snake lamp by Edgar Brandt is one of Joseph's favourite pieces. He has had it for 15 years and it moves with him wherever he goes.

Joseph's enthusiasm for Liaigre knows no bounds. 'The design and furniture by Liaigre are what I like most about our home. I knew that the traditional house, which was originally built in the 1930s and which had all its authentic features, could be brought to life again through Christian's eyes. I wanted it to have a "mature" feel: beautiful wood, rich colours but to retain the clean lines that I love so much. It does have a much more relaxed feel than any of my working environments; it is softer and the fact that the lighting is more subdued adds to its warmth. I don't need a professional kind of environment here: I restrict any work I do at home just to thinking.'

Joseph moved to the Chelsea house where he lives with his wife and daughter early in 1995, from an apartment that could not cope with the arrival of Gigi, their exuberant first child. 'We wanted a space that was more suitable for a family. Having lived in an apartment for many years, we liked the idea of a house and of living on different levels. Its previous occupants had also been a family. You can sense this, and it gives a good feeling. Our kitchen has a dining table where we entertain informally and where the family can eat. This has made it the heart of the house – something that was missing from our previous apartment, which had no real core. We also have a "den" which is a great little hideaway, somewhere where I can be on my own if I need to be – particularly if Chelsea FC are playing!

'I have been told that the interior is a little unexpected. It is certainly unique and naturally this is also something one tries to achieve when putting together a new collection. Being involved in designing a house is like designing anything, though: no matter how wonderful the initial idea is, there are always

Above left: A Joseph breakfast – cigarette, coffee and Oreos – with a coffee set that dates from the 1930s. Above right: A doorway in sycamore wood frames a leather sofa with raw silk covers. The low table is ebony and the statue is a Shona piece from West Africa.

practical considerations to work around. Being a designer myself means that interiors are important to me – it's about getting it right for *me*.' Joseph's ideas about what is right for him are – understandably – pretty specific. Before he met his wife, they notably revolved around an austere high-tech Eva Jiricna flat and lots of black designer suits from Comme des Garçons and Yohji Yamamoto. When Isabel came into his life, and after their marriage, Joseph's wardrobe suddenly began to veer more towards tailor-made Italian white linen suits. 'She lightens me up,' he explains. Meanwhile, his new wife was trying to cover up the chrome and black leather furniture under casually draped textiles. Joseph realized that it was time to move.

In order to avoid marital arguments on questions of style, Joseph brought in Liaigre, who has both a designer's edge in his decorative projects and a certain warmth in his materials. These two high priests of chic thought long and hard about all the various possibilities. Wood was to be the main ingredient bringing *noblesse* and texture. The plans settled, Joseph agreed to use Liaigre's own team of French carpenters and so Isabel and Gigi were dispatched to France for a holiday while the carpenters took over: 'a little cultural exchange', as Joseph describes it. While the carpenters were completely re-building the ground floor Joseph stoically confined himself to the top of the house, viewing the progress morning and evening and generally becoming 'incredibly involved'.

Left: In the TV room: a 1940s sofa opposite a pair of 1950s chairs. The parchment-top tables are by Leleu, Paris. The painting is by Robert Motherwell, while the bronze banjo player came from a Paris flea market. The linen carpet is by Liaigre. Above: A detail of a Joseph leather jacket.

'Interiors are important to me – it's about getting it right for *me*.'

The resulting space is fantastic: much more flexible than most London family houses. It has been designed so that the light from the original lead-paned windows is coaxed right into the house; wherever you are, there is a perspective of a window. Liaigre managed this with two big ebony-lined arches and a wood-and-glass partition that successfully brings a great feeling of modernity to the space, despite his claims about having been inspired by Anglo-colonial interiors like Raffles Hotel in Singapore. This romantic influence is visible only in the choice of dark wood, and in the lines of certain pieces of furniture, such as the 'Joe' chair. Like the 'Gigi' sofa, the chairs form part of the barrage of special pieces designed by Liaigre specifically for the house. So the king of ready-to-wear retailing has a home that could only qualify as couture? Joseph smiles. 'My home is somewhere I can relax completely, and that is all that matters.'

Above left and right: Two details from Joseph collections that demonstrate the classic qualities of one of England's most fashionable designers.
Right: The bed, designed by Christian Liaigre. The bed linen was brought back from a trip to America.

KENZO

Where, you might ask, are the flowers? Kenzo is the fashion world's undisputed flower king, who discovered fashion during flower power, and who has never strayed from the garden path. Yet in the 10,000 square feet of his Parisian home, there is no trace of a plate scattered with carnations, or a curtain sown with forget-me-nots, designs he has produced for his Kenzo Maison line. When the front door opens, in this shabby Parisian courtyard, tucked away behind the Bastille, it opens on to another world. Everything inside is sumptuous but understated: blond wood, gently trickling water, Zen. Take off your shoes as you arrive chez Kenzo, because you are crossing from the West into the Orient, and it is quite an abrupt transition.

Kenzo is quite happy to send out on the runway a patchwork jacket with a brocade waistcoat, a flowered tie, a patterned shirt and a checked scarf. He himself dresses in tweeds coupled with lavender sweaters and chintz mufflers – few can mix and match as he does. But could it be that the debonair and nonchalant Kenzo, known fondly as 'the most Parisian of the Japanese', harbours a secret homesickness behind the famous smile, a little dose of nostalgia for his mother country? 'Well, it does hit me sometimes, especially at weekends,' he admits ruefully, 'and although I am not very Zen myself, I really wanted a completely serene home. I am a lapsed student of Zen ... but I still wanted to feel it around me.' Kenzo grins, slightly abashed, from under his floppy hair. He used to be one of Paris's great party-givers and has a reputation of really knowing how to enjoy himself; he has, as one friend has described it, 'a Latin attitude in an Oriental physique'.

Opening pages: Five Imari porcelain vases contrast with a bright orange outfit from the summer 1996 men's collection. Left: The swimming pool.
Above left: The Japanese sitting room with day beds by Liaigre, a Chinese lacquer table and Japanese porcelain. Above right: The Zen garden.

Kenzo's celebrated happy-go-lucky disposition, reflected in his colourful clothes, perhaps comes from having been born into beauty. His father ran a traditional tea house in the Japanese provinces and, as a child, Kenzo would see the kimono-sellers come round each season with their gaily patterned wares. His sister lent him her fashion magazines and Kenzo set to work – on doll's clothes. His parents refused to allow him to train as a fashion designer, because they did not consider it a suitable profession for a young man. But determined, Kenzo left for Tokyo. He went to night school and followed correspondence courses to master the rudiments of fashion design, supporting himself by working as an assistant to a painter. Forty years later the brushstrokes of Kenzo's troubled beginnings are still evident in his collections, and his desk is littered with rainbows of pencils, ready to colour the world. Eventually he managed to enrol in the prestigious Bunk Fashion School which had taken the momentous decision to accept a few boys. Having completed the course, and with diplomas and prizes in his pocket, Kenzo then unexpectedly hit the jackpot: a pay-off from a developer who wanted to buy him out of his Tokyo apartment.

He immediately took the slow boat to Paris with his head full of dreams and a pocket providentially full of money. Hong Kong, Saigon, Singapore, Colombo, Djibouti, Alexandria, Barcelona ... a long month's sailing, a train, and finally he ended up in the cold and the grey of a run-down hotel on the Left Bank. Where were the parties? The beautifully dressed women? Endless spring? Paris was jaded and, pre-1968,

it offered no answers. The *allure* and charisma that had reached out to him from the pages of the French magazines in Tokyo did not seem to exist. Perhaps it is as a direct response to that initial disappointment that on Kenzo's catwalk it is nearly always eternal spring, with orange and red and green and yellow acting as his navy blue. Perhaps he is still insistent about supplying Paris with a glamour that he felt so keenly to be wanting on his arrival.

'Although it may not seem so at first sight, the house is like my fashion: it has absorbed an infinite number of influences, what in French is called a *métissage*. I have done collections that featured kimonos, and collections that featured flamenco dresses, gypsy skirts, cowboy costumes, bou-bous, saris ... I love to travel and I'm just as likely to pick up an idea for a collection while I'm away as I am one for the house.'

Things have calmed down significantly, however, since the death a few years ago of his close associate and partner Xavier de Castella. They had designed the house together on a grand scale, with architect Kenji Kawabata. It occupies the site of a

disused warehouse and today boasts three levels, five terraces and a breathtaking Japanese garden, cleverly designed to appear much larger than the 1,600 square feet that it actually occupies. All the earth for the garden had to be brought in, as did the authentic Japanese cherry tree. 'The plants mostly came from Hamburg, from Europe's largest nursery, but the bamboo came from the south of France because I wanted big plants. Japanese plants do quite well in the Parisian climate, and the garden is now mature. We moved in 1990, but it took three and a half years to finish the house and garden properly.'

Left: The oak steps leading from the sitting room to the dining room illustrate the expansive and abundant use of this wood throughout the house.
Above: A view of the Japanese dining room with traditionally low seats and table. In the background, Kenzo is spelled out in Japanese calligraphy.

'Colours are one way to bring joy; Zen is

There is one section of the house which is purely Japanese: tatami mats on the floor and sliding rice-paper doors, with lots of highly polished wood and a black jacuzzi that looks like a ritual pool. The only furniture comprises a few low tables and a few equally low chairs; everything can be quickly pushed aside to make way for a futon, and life can be lived pretty much exactly as it would be in traditional Japan, with a view of cherry blossom and the sacred carp through the window. 'It's actually quite like being in Japan, except that the chef is French, and he hasn't quite got that Japanese touch.'

Previous pages: The room that houses the jacuzzi, with its walls of wood and slate, looks out on to the bamboo garden. Above left: The bathroom, where mirrors multiply the room's bold lines and emphasize the abundant light. Above right: An Oriental sculpture from Kenzo's extensive collection.

another ... the goal is happiness and serenity.'

Then, as there is another side to Kenzo, there is the other part of the house, where French eighteenth-century beds are upholstered in funky black leather, and contemporary paintings of Native Americans hang beside a luscious turquoise indoor swimming pool and engravings of Napoleon's campaign in Egypt.

The pleasurable cacophony of colours and patterns that characterizes Kenzo's fashion seems a long way from his oak and cream interior. 'But colours are one way to bring joy; Zen is another. It all boils down to the same thing. In both cases the goal is happiness and serenity.'

Above: The bedroom with its open Japanese-style fireplace, which has chain-mesh fireguard curtains. The floor is covered in traditional tatami mats. The sliding doors are of rice paper, linen and glass.

MICHEL KLEIN

One of the most interesting facets of Michel Klein's disposition is the contrast he maintains between the vivid colours and exuberant style of his various homes, and his minimalist approach to fashion. Because he is the handsome young darling of the French press, both have been widely reported, and while his collections remain monochromatic exercises in purity, his idyllic *mas* in Provence and his apartments in Paris have continued to be vibrantly coloured. The walls appear to have been happily daubed by a child high on a dizzying palette of Caran d'Ache finger paints. The reality is not far removed, for Klein confesses to a 'colour rush' every time he passes under the lintel of Sennelier, the chic artist's suppliers on the Left Bank in Paris: 'When I see the tones, the dyes, the powders ... I just want to buy and use them all!'

Klein tells the story of a celebrated French journalist who went to visit him recently in Provence and asked: 'How can someone like you, whose fashion lacks the slightest touch of colour, be capable of putting so much colour on your walls? If only you could do with fashion what you do with your houses.'

Opening pages: A Klein waistcoat and jacket and his specially made wrought-iron bed. Above left: A Chinese jacket by Klein on a nineteenth-century armchair. Above right: One of a pair of crystal candlesticks, a gift from photographer Bettina Rheims. Right: The sitting room, once Vuillard's atelier.

Right: The small dining room was painted red to give it dignity. It has the same leopardskin moquette as the home office.

Far right: The caramel linen curtains in the office offset the paint effects on the wall and add to the neutral colour scheme.

'If I did with fashion what I do with houses, women would look stupid!' retorts Klein, quite legitimately piqued. 'They would look like parrots – which I don't consider the most beautiful things on earth. So few people can get away with wearing eccentric clothes: Loulou de la Falaise is probably the only person I know who can wear pink, purple and yellow together and still look chic. Wearing multicoloured clothes hides the personality; whereas black makes you more ... radiant. It is partly because I make monochromatic clothes that I like having colourful houses. Recently people have been dressing more flashily and it's just awful when they come here. Heavily decorated houses suit soberly dressed people best.'

The apartment that Klein inhabits now has a room in every colour: red for the intimate dining room, porcelain blue for the *salon*, beige and leopardskin for the study. 'The study had to be neutral because that's where I choose fabric for the collections. Just try doing it in a room with blue walls: it's impossible. Other colours look quite different, especially in artificial light. It's a shame really because the main room has beautiful, steady, north light – painters' light.'

There is a happy coincidence attached to the fact that Klein is now the tenant of this two-storey artist's atelier, rich in nineteenth-century period detailing. It once belonged to Edouard Vuillard, an Impressionist artist celebrated for his poetic studies of interiors and cityscapes. 'Vuillard had always been my favourite painter. When I was living on the Quai Voltaire, the gallery that houses most of his work was close by and I would often pop in to browse. One day I was sitting in the lounge and I saw something out of the corner of my eye that reminded me eerily of a Vuillard painting I knew. It was a really strange feeling of *déjà-vu*.

'It is partly because I make monochromatic clothes that I like having colourful houses.'

Eventually I realized that there were several paintings that depicted the view of the square from this window. I asked the owner, and it transpired that Vuillard had lived here for about 15 years. It was a very joyful moment. It's quite something to realize that you have unknowingly ended up living in the home of the painter you most admire. It made me feel that I had been right about taking it.'

His first visit had been pretty inauspicious. 'The flat was advertised rather laconically in *Le Figaro* as "atelier d'artiste, Clichy", or something like that. It was a bit sinister: really dirty, dark red carpet on the floor, beige walls. It was squalid and looked as if nobody had lived here for years. There were some incredible features, though: the marble doorframes, the huge fireplace, the double-height window, and the two storeys that made it feel like a house ... even if it was all buried under layers of dirt.'

The major renovation work Klein undertook here signalled a new departure for the designer. 'I found the apartment just when I was starting to work in haute couture for the house of Guy Laroche, and I very much felt that I wanted to do something grand – excessive even. I didn't want this to be just another

Above left and right: The bedroom with its Wedgwood-effect blue-and-white colour scheme, which exploits the attractive period mouldings. Blue-and-white Delft tiles around the fireplace develop the theme.

apartment in my life. For the first time, I really wanted an apartment to be properly finished ... I wanted colours to be specially created and mixed. The way I set about decorating was exactly the way I set about doing a couture collection – commissioning real artists and artisans. I designed my own bed and had an *artisan ferronier* (who had just made me an armature for a couture dress) make it. The leopardskin design for the carpet upstairs is a pattern we magnified from a fabric from the haute couture collection. It was very amusing. You can do a house like a collection, but only by using those few elements that will withstand the seasons: a dress can be transient while you have to live with a house for a long time.'

When asked if the house would have looked the same without the input of his fashion experience, Klein replies with a twinkle in his eye: 'The problem with that question is that if I hadn't been doing fashion, I would certainly have been doing houses. One must keep elements of bad taste – the fashion elements. A house must never be perfect or static, and it must never give the impression that it will always stay the same. I like places that you can add and add to ... I just love doing houses.'

Above centre: One of a pair of small white chairs. It is made entirely out of horseshoes and is a good example of 1950s popular art.
Above right: Klein is fond of the contrast between modern art, such as this painting by Olivier Venard, and delicate antiques.

KOJI

The young Japanese designer Koji Tatsuno dreams up shapes out of fabric as fine as gossamer, out of net and mirror and paper, and precious metallic weaves. The textiles are often highly sophisticated synthetic amalgams, or conversely, exquisite handmade collages of materials as diverse as lurex, plastic, rubber and raffia. He seems to have plucked his inspiration from the natural world; here a spider's web of gold thread, there a honeycomb cape, a gown of multicoloured petals, a bunch of algae that is a skirt, and, hanging on the wall, a length of fabric that evokes sun on the sea – all gorgeous stuff. In a sense it is cyber-fashion, haute couture for a flower princess of the twenty-first century.

Koji occupies a unique place in the fashion firmament because he is an incurable romantic, who enfolds his models in calyx-like whorls of glamorous silks. But at the same time he has a hands-on approach that defines him as somehow beyond fashion, a sculptor of the unusual medium he has chosen to adopt. He moulds the body, rips, twists, wrinkles and folds the fabric to create completely new textures. He works with heat-sensitive yarns, high-tech stuffs, feathers, sequins and gauze. Within the context of the fashion world he appears as a conceptual artist, although he would never describe himself as one.

Opening pages: A leather club armchair sprayed gold, and a detail of a ruffled golden raffia cape. Above left: A Fortuny lamp with a chair by Scott Crolla. Above right: Photographs from the Natural History Museum, New York and a flea-market sofa. Right: The music system and flea-market finds.

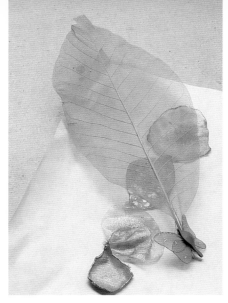

'I think the home

By definition, fashion designers make clothes – to be worn, sold, marketed. Yet to call Koji's one-off pieces 'clothes' is to understate his esoteric imaginings. He seems to have managed to preserve his vision from mundane considerations, despite many of his creations being considered unwearable and others being too delicate to reproduce. The unique pieces are a very modern luxury, close to the maddest moment of the golden age of couture, or to the inspired costumes for the eccentric balls of the 1930s. His creations appeal to the senses, and are both largely uncontrollable and inaccessible to the hard-nosed critical intelligence that governs the conventional fashion system.

'When I started in the fashion business, I didn't make a conscious decision to become a fashion designer or anything like that. In fact, it all happened by chance. I had to leave home at the age of 14, so I didn't go to high school. In Japan, if you don't go to high school it's impossible to find any work, and equally impossible, of course, to be admitted to any specialist school. I wanted to go to art school but obviously they wouldn't take me, so in a way there was nothing for me in Japan. A friend suggested London and I thought, "Why not? – there is no future for me here." So I came, just like that.

'I didn't know anybody, and I didn't really speak English either, so I just survived from day to day. If I managed to build up something, it was out of desperation. At around this time – it was when I was 18 or 19 – I found a bit of traditional kimono fabric, and made a shirt for myself, because I literally didn't have the money to buy clothes. One day, when I was wearing the shirt, somebody stopped me in the street to ask me where I had got it and I told him that I had made it myself. That person was a buyer from Browns, who then asked me to make some to sell in the shop, and it all took off from there.'

Nowadays, after riding the swings and roundabouts of the complex world of fashion financing, and having undertaken the eternal search for a backer that all truly innovative designers have to come to terms with, Koji has become independent. He shows a limited collection of about 12 pieces during the Paris

Above: A catwalk shot, with samples of handmade 'petals and leaves' – for possible use in the collection. **Right:** In the foreground are a Charles Eames chair and a psychedelic 1970s carpet from the flea market. Koji's workbench is embellished with his collection of butterfly images.

should be personally inspiring.'

ready-to-wear collections. While some get snapped up by collectors, some are sold in his made-to-measure boutique; others end up decorating the walls of the Parisian loft where he lives with his girlfriend. The loft is where Koji set up his studio when he moved to Paris from London in the mid-1990s: 'It is in the Bastille area, in the 11th arrondissement, which is full of people of all different nationalities. It's a less sophisticated and "developed" part of Paris – vibrant and multicultural.'

Koji's pad vibrates to the house, techno and trance music that he prefers. As a home it is extremely laid back, bohemian to a fault – to the point that it boasts the archetypal mattress on the floor. It is the kind of place that most consecrated fashion designers wouldn't dream of living in after leaving art school – even for a day. Koji himself, who makes some of the most fragile, precious gowns around, insists that the discrepancy is not so great as it may seem.

'When my clothes *are* worn, and sometimes, I admit, they are unique and pretty ethereal, I would still prefer that they be worn with everyday things, and not kept for special occasions. I think that this is a more contemporary attitude. You can have precious possessions but still treat them as everyday things. That is the way that we live today, isn't it? And that is why, when I have paintings – or indeed dresses – in the house, I don't want to hide them away or make them into precious objects; I want them to become part of my life. Clothes are to wear, and the house is somewhere you spend a great deal of your time, so there is a strong link between the two. I love doing an apartment or house; it's great fun, it's just another extension of a visual experiment.'

Opposite left: The bedroom, with two dresses – designed for Spring–Summer 1993 – hanging from the ceiling.

Opposite centre: A typical Koji creation.

Opposite right: Another view of the bedroom. The bed is covered with a textile from India. The sofa has been sprayed with gold paint, and the low armchair is upholstered in a silk-pleated fabric by Koji.

Left: A length of cotton gauze, to which Koji himself applied iridescent plastic, to make a backdrop for an exhibition.

Above: The 'Butterfly' cape, designed by Koji for Peter Greenaway's film *The Pillow Book*. The chandelier was a flea-market find (with Christmas baubles still attached).

Right: The gold-sprayed armchair is draped with an Indian textile and two Moroccan cushion covers. On the right the safe, which is original to the space, has been sprayed silver. The photograph on the left was picked up on the street, whereas the religious icons were bought in the south of France. The shelves house part of Koji's vast reference library.

He does a lot of work at home, sketching or researching, sitting at the kitchen table, surrounded by an eclectic selection of objects. 'I like all sorts of things, anything I can relate to on a personal level. I never set out to collect, or to decorate as such. I don't have a specific topic or theme that I collect around, or anything like that. It's when I travel that I tend to pick things up. I collect things that remind me of other people, experiences. Often people give me presents, so I relate to the object on a personal level – it reminds me of the circumstances in which I was given it. I think the home should be personally inspiring, and that's why I have lots of small bits and pieces around which don't mean anything to anybody else – because they all signify something to me. It's romantic, and my clothes are like that too, in a way. They have the same sort of personality as my home. My own, probably.

'I feel the clothes that I design and the house that I live in are on the same wavelength: it has something to do with catching the light – I love reflections, and anything to do with light, so I play around with light as much as possible. I'll weave glitter or sequins into a textile for a dress in the same way that I place little sources of light around the house.'

Koji is preoccupied by light, space, purity and spontaneity; they apply equally to his fashion, to his quirky furniture designs, upholstered in handmade fabric, and to the unostentatious, free-flowing space where he lives. In France they call him '*le poète*', and indeed he lives as only a poet could.

Above: The kitchen area, with its standard cabinets and with the table covered with a sari. It is here that Koji tends to spend most of his time, sketching. The chairs are simple office chairs. Pinned on the far wall is a pleated 'Honeycomb' shawl designed by Koji.

BEN DE LISI

Ben de Lisi has a short name, almost minimalist, that gives a lot away. Firstly 'Ben': efficient, American and to the point; then 'de Lisi', speaking volumes about good-looking and excitable Italian immigrants who make New York what it is. The man behind the name comes from Brooklyn, and is reputedly as temperamental, enthusiastic and vociferous as any self-respecting Sicilian. Yet he creates clothes that radiate calm, with the quiet sexiness that has made contemporary American ready-to-wear so strong. It is quite a combination: de Lisi's perfectly cut but understated fashion has taken England by storm. He is on a self-proclaimed one-man mission to bring chic (in the New York sense of the word) to the banks of the River Thames. 'It seems to me', he says with the bedside manner of a slightly wacky doctor, 'that there is a great need for someone to provide women with these kinds of clothes.' By doing so, he has recently run away with the British Fashion Glamour Award – twice. One season he had the even more glamorous idea of putting Britpop babe Patsy Kensit (a long-standing fan) on his catwalk – to the delight of the paparazzi. He has, in fact, dressed almost all the British stars and starlets of the 1990s; they are attracted to the subtle but addictive modernity of his clothes.

De Lisi has been living in London since 1980, drawn to its cosmopolitan atmosphere. He lives in a very grey, un-English apartment building; not just any apartment building, though, it is on the King's Road, and one that features underground parking and an amiable doorman – very 'New York'. The view, however, with the River Thames snaking across from the Houses of Parliament to Battersea Bridge is unequivocally London. 'I had been looking for months, and the estate agents were continually showing me poky dark

Opening pages: A detail of a de Lisi dress, the stripes echoed in the 1950s Danish ceramic bottles. Left: A corner of the sitting room looking towards the kitchen, which is separated by a walnut-veneered partition. Black lino runs thoughout the apartment. Above: Jugs by Dansk.

'This apartment ... is an extension of what I

basement flats in the outer reaches. When I saw the light and the view from here, it was irresistible. If people come and visit – although with a cream carpet I don't tempt fate by having too many parties – they are always surprised to find a flat like this in such a boring-looking building. The block was designed purely by the developers' greed, with no questions asked about harmony or proportion. The flat itself, however, is not austere but beautiful and simple. I like the fact that it is exactly like living in a hotel and that it looks after itself. I moved here at the end of a relationship that had lasted 15 years; I needed a change, and I opted for the smaller place but the better location. Chelsea is very familiar to me. Everything is at my fingertips here: shops, cinemas, restaurants.'

Above left: Adam Dolle designed the sofa and the birch plywood cube next to it. The pottery is by Hornsea and the 1956 coffee table is by Poul Kjaerholm, inspired by Mies van der Rohe. Above right: A David Bands painting above a limed oak 1940s American table. The 1950s lamp is by Knoll.

do: very pure, understated and rich in detail.'

He loves minimalism, but not the cold, restrained kind, and this is apparent both in his fashion and his home. The flat was entirely redesigned for him by fellow New Yorker Adam Dolle. But before Dolle was allowed to attack the laminates, hessian walls and latticework radiator screens, the designer sent him to look at his clothes. Patently, Dolle understood the de Lisi fashion aesthetic to perfection, and the box-like apartment is now characterized by the kind of blasé chic that de Lisi is used to in his customers. The 1970s existing laminates were replaced by elegant American walnut veneer, and the tiny apartment was structured so that both the bedroom and hallway are dark, allowing the main space – an expanse of cream – to dazzle and dominate. The terrace, with its breathtaking view, leads right off it. Visually, this

Above centre: A detail of a Ben de Lisi fabric. Above right: On the balcony are two 1950s 'diamond' chairs, designed by Harry Bertoia for Knoll. The superb view of London from the balcony was the main reason why de Lisi moved into the apartment.

manipulation of dark and light is rewarding. The contrast between the dark wood-panelled corridor and the luminous living room makes the apartment appear much larger than its scant 550 square feet.

None of London's infamous 'shabby chic' has influenced his home: the pared-down lines of vintage designs are thrown into sharp relief by the natural light which spills in from the south-facing windows. It is a clutter-free zone, in the same way that his clothes are free from excess adornment and simply play on the body and the luxury of the best fabric.

The decorative palette is de Lisi's signature coffee, chocolate and cream – the colours around which he often builds his catwalk collections. The furniture comprises a wise selection of modern classics: a sofa made out of two Knoll chairs upholstered in flannel and bouclé wool, a Marcel Breuer table, Arne Jacobsen and Charles Eames chairs, Scandinavian ceramics, Bauhaus lamps. As with his clothing, de Lisi's taste veers towards furniture that is assured, focused and restrained. 'I would rather live without it if it's not the right piece; in my experience, it's usually only worth having if you can't afford it! As with fashion, it is more difficult to keep things simple than to be excessive, but I wanted things to be very twentieth century, and very me – I'm single now and this apartment reflects totally my own imprint. It is an extension of what I do: very pure, understated and rich in detail. "Keep it simple" is my motto.' The apartment admirably reflects this creed, and London might just be ready for that quintessential de Lisi appreciation of simple elegance, pared down to the most beautiful of basics, and applied to interiors.

Above: A stacking dresser in the bedroom: 'a box on a box on a box' designed by Dolle, who was inspired by the work of Charles Eames.
Right: A painting by David Bands hangs over a cashmere-upholstered bedhead. The table and the blankets are by Conran.

ANGELA MISSONI

With naughty nut-brown eyes and a kitsch, flamboyant fashion sense, Angela Missoni is a fashion princess. She has recently propelled the family firm into the stratosphere of utter trendiness. Characteristically kaleidoscopic Missoni knits, lusted after by twentysomethings who missed the 1970s the first time around, are today experiencing a stylistic revival. It is the best sort of revival too, because what Angela Missoni and her team of international arbiters of cool are doing is trying to evoke such high moments of style as the first ever Missoni show in 1966, when ultra-modern models with shorn heads wore Biba-style mini-dresses. The following year, even more futuristically, the models floated round a pool on transparent inflatable furniture for the Missoni fashion 'happening'. Angela, as the eldest daughter, had quite a tradition to live up to.

Missoni became a label in 1953 when Angela's mother Rosita was barely 21. The daughter of a well-established weaver, she had just married the handsome Ottavio Missoni, who had run for Italy in the 1948 Olympics, despite having just spent four years in a prisoner-of-war camp in Egypt. He was interested in applying the weaving process to sportswear, so together the young couple began to design, incorporating the colours they both loved into the recipe. The rest, as they say, is history, and since 1997 the business has been officially in Angela's hands. 'I was a little worried that we were going to have a Prince Charles effect,' she smiles, 'because my parents are still so active. I thought that perhaps they would not be ready to give up until my children were ready to take over.'

Opening pages: Part of the Dan Friedman screen and a view of the veranda. Above left: Colourful Missoni knits. Above right: A Guelfenbein painting hangs in the dining room, above the piano left to Angela by her grandmother. The 'totems' are by Roger Selden. Right: Flowers: fake, real and in buttons.

It is not only for her three children that Angela has stayed in Sumirago, a small and very green village in the foothills of the Alps near the town of Varese, an area famous for its weaving dynasties. She is surrounded by rolling hills and lakes and the homes of other members of the Missoni clan (Rosita Missoni had 13 cousins). Although to the outsider's eye it may seem surprising that Angela – exuberant, international and sociable – lives in the country, a good hour's drive from the nearest club, she is invested with family values, and the Missonis all work together in the family factory five minutes' drive up the road: 'Sometimes I feel that that's my real home.' Angela often sees her parents and two brothers for lunch and

Above: A view of the sitting room, with its informal atmosphere and its tiled floor, which helps to keep the house cool in summer. Part of Angela Missoni's collection of kitsch bits and pieces from all over the world is on display.

at weekends, despite the fact that they already spend all their working day together. They are so clannish that for years Missoni's advertising was a photograph of the family – numbering up to 20 of them. Angela was much moved when she discovered old photographs showing one of her mother's cousins playing in the grounds of what is now her house. It is attached to the apartment where she lived as a girl, and her father owns the land – originally bought because of the fine trees. Family, for the Missonis, is everything.

Angela moved into the late nineteenth-century villa when her third child was born. It had been rather unsuccessfully renovated in the 1960s, and she decided to re-work the spaces completely, adding a floor, repairing a roof and puncturing the façade with much-needed windows. She built a veranda to bring some of the voluptuous greenery inside and painted the whole place in dove grey, which acts as a neutral foil to her eclectic collection of objects.

'At 20 you don't listen to architects. Sometimes I rather wish I had, because now I have this huge house and only five rooms.' Angela stands in her kitchen, the only room that looks

Above: A colourful Memphis table by Michele de Lucchi, a wedding gift, below a large canvas by Eduardo Guelfenbein, representing a party in Sydney. The wooden palm tree on the left is a souvenir from Bali.

'The house has the same qualities that I draw upon for my mad patterns and crazy colourways.'

rationally designed. 'I love food and I love to cook, so the kitchen was important and I was terrified of getting it wrong. We all camped in the attic and cooked on a gas ring for two years!' The attic, a loft-like room of 16,000 square feet, with fantastic views over the Monte Rosa, was conceived as Angela's 'grown-up world: my bedroom, bathroom and my own sitting room. I was influenced by the idea of one large space, with no doors.' The only dividers are Japanese-style screens that glide across, studded with a rich patchwork of family snapshots. The children's rooms are on the floor below and the dining room

Above: Two views of Angela's luxurious bathroom. A collection of nudes hangs by the jacuzzi. The original barber's chair was bought at a flea market; it is much used, as Angela cuts the whole family's hair.

is by the stairs going down to the ground floor. That room is dominated by a very 'New York' Dan Friedman screen, while the lounge boasts a large painting by Chilean artist Eduardo Guelfenbein. His vibrant colourful brushstrokes are the artistic reflection not only of the Missoni rainbow palette but also of Angela's interior, depending as that does for its effect on sudden flashes of colour: a Memphis table here, a giant wooden palm tree from Bali there, a collection of 1950s glass baubles. Angela Missoni's home has no proper structuring of space, but it has vitality and movement. It feels spontaneous much as the clothes she designs. 'I wanted to create a house that was in the country without being a country house. I wanted something modern, something new. I don't have any proper furniture, just chairs and sofas from flea markets. For me the biggest link between my fashion designing and the interior is that the moment I began to design seriously, I stopped taking care of the house. Nowadays I just have weekend blitzes!

'The other link is that the house is full of Missoni clothes. Although I don't design at home, I do wear the result! Seriously, I suppose the house has the same intuitive and spontaneous qualities that I draw upon for my mad patterns and crazy colourways.' An outsider can spot the link immediately: Angela's house has been funky for years, and now she has begun to apply that approach to the company.

Above: A view of the master bedroom, which is separated from the en-suite bathroom only by the sliding Japanese-style door. The embroidered bed cover came from Rajasthan, and the bedside tables are Shaker. A Madonna and Child painting hangs over the bed.

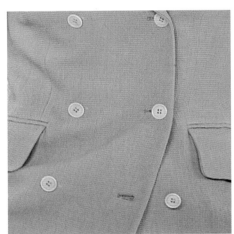

ISAAC MIZRAHI

Everything about Isaac Mizrahi is excessive. Even by his late twenties he had New York's Seventh Avenue in thrall and was quickly christened 'Miz the Whiz' by the influential trade rag *Women's Wear Daily* (WWD). He won three coveted Designer of the Year awards during his first five years in business, and is now rapidly expanding in Asia in what WWD classified as a 'mega-move'; forever apt, they have long declared everyone 'in a tizzy over Izzy'. Such a success story is very New York, and Mizrahi is the quintessential New Yorker, with his Brooklyn accent and good Jewish boy's education. He is flamboyant and camp in a *bon-enfant* kind of way. He is kitsch, effusive, unstoppable. He is affectionate, self-mocking, loyal, and very, very funny. He has an army of friends who 'adore' him, and the kind of interests that in England you might expect of a rather well-to-do dowager: bridge, Bach and ballet.

Vogue has singled out Mizrahi as one of fashion's new Establishment, laying bets that he will be a household name by the end of the decade. In America he is already just that – in the better dressed households at any rate – due to the brilliant 1995 documentary film *Unzipped*, which starred Mizrahi and his world. *Unzipped* scooped up film awards, but, unexpectedly, it also generated huge affection for the eccentric prodigy. It had a phenomenal effect on his popularity, probably because Mizrahi came across as a thoroughly good guy – extravagant, perhaps, but in full possession of a sharp sense of humour too.

In real life, Mizrahi speaks in capital letters, and has quirky grammar, thick with adjectives, which reflects an infectious enthusiasm for everything he does. It is this deep-seated sense of fun that lies behind the brilliant colours (inspired, he admits, by candy wrappers) and mad prints of his signature collections.

Opening pages: A detail of the buttoning on a Mizrahi double-breasted jacket, and the dining table set for dinner beneath a junk-store chandelier. The designer is fond of extraordinary junk, such as the 1950s patio chairs. Right: A Vertès screen behind Isaac's pride and joy: his 1930s Steinway piano.

One is reminded of the 1950s 'fashion-goes-to-Hollywood' musical comedy *Funny Face*, and the editors' war cry: 'Banish the black...think pink.' If there is ever to be a remake, Mizrahi would be spot-on in the

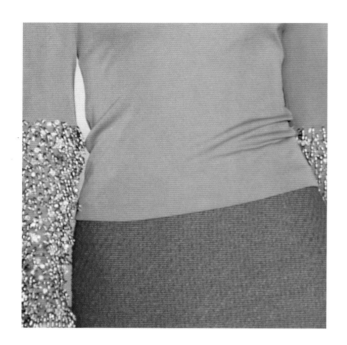

barmy Kay Thompson role – a good-time, pseudo-Diana Vreeland. He would no doubt qualify, having studied acting and music at the High School of Performing Arts. He combined his coursework with evening classes in fashion at the equally renowned Parson's School of Design. After his graduation as an actor in 1979, he enrolled at Parson's full time. Mizrahi had known even when he was 12 that he wanted to be a designer, ever since watching a 1960s television remake about the thwarted love affair of a fashion designer. High heels, taffeta, lengths of silk: he was smitten ... while his Yeshiva teachers could not understand why the odd little boy insisted on making dresses for Barbie.

The essential thing to grasp about Mizrahi is his deep-seated admiration for all the great glamour moments. He seems to have the entire catalogue at his fingertips, like the curator of the MGM film library, and he positively melts at the idea of Audrey Hepburn's graphic minimalism or Rita Hayworth's satin-clad Gilda. His mother, who got her Norell dresses and the like at Loehman's and who has a great original sense of style, is part of all that. 'She dared to wear my father's pyjamas to the beach before anyone had thought of it ... a connoisseur.' Both Mizrahi and his mother understandably shed tears when they discovered – after he had moved in – that Norell had previously lived in Isaac's new apartment building. Strangely, the decorative scheme that Mizrahi and his architect Ross Anderson had outlined drew heavily on Norell – bleached wood and natural leather. With such serendipitous beginnings, the tiny Greenwich Village apartment still charms him: 'It was my life's dream to live in the Village. All my needs are satisfied by this apartment. It is the perfect size ... I'm too busy really for a grand place.' Nevertheless, Mizrahi often entertains friends: 'I prefer intimate groups, and considering the size of the apartment, it's a good thing.'

Although Anderson had also collaborated on Mizrahi's atelier, the apartment was slower to mature, even though all they really did was tidy up the interior. 'I wanted something soothing. Cosy. Easy. My life is complicated and I need respite from it. I did not want anything that required too much maintenance.

Previous pages: Everything on the wall behind the piano holds some special significance for the designer. Above: A 1997 Mizrahi outfit. Right: The dining room becomes an atelier when the Ross Anderson tabletop is exchanged for a drawing board, using an old medical cabinet as a base.

'The same sensibility reverberates in all

The re-definition of luxury is consistent with what I did in the atelier: the mix of raw and refined elements and textures. It was not until I got my piano, which is the central element in my apartment, that I could decorate. I knew it would dominate and I knew it was senseless to proceed with anything else in the room. I lived like a monk until it came. I practically even waited to unpack – considering the piano took two and a half years to find, that was very slow progress. A German Steinway of circa 1936, it is my most prized possession: pristine ivories, perfect tone, heavenly action.'

Once the piano was installed, Mizrahi set about seeking out furniture for his decorative theme: 'Fred Astaire meets *2001 – A Space Odyssey*'. Looking at the apartment's clean lines and classic design pieces, Astaire seems to have come out tops. 'Everything I choose is me. I think that because I am a fashion

Above left: The 'long and skinny' terrace which, Mizrahi says, has taught him to enjoy the summer months, and enthusiastically to cultivate gardenias.
Above right: The bedroom, where the bed with integral drawers is by Ross Anderson. The standard lamp by the window is by Noguchi.

that I do – whether it's a room or a suit.'

designer I am less fearful about experimenting at home. And, acting as an arbiter of fashion, you have answers for lots of design queries. But knowing how many options there are can confuse the issue. And yet everything I do relates to everything else. I can't say how specifically: suffice it to say that the same sensibility reverberates in all that I do – whether it's a room, or a suit, or a soufflé, or a piano concerto.

'Days are rarely typical in my life. The only constant is what I eat for breakfast. When I work at home I shuffle between the drawing table and the piano. Something about practising the piano while I'm designing clothes works for me. I like to do many things at once. My favourite thing is to be in the bath, with the bedroom door open so that I can see the television (or its mirror image). I also spend a lot of time in bed, which is where I have the most fun – whether I am alone or accompanied.'

Above left: A detail of a clean, sharp pea-coat lapel. Above right: Not only is the bed high off the ground, the effect is compounded by the bedroom ceiling being lower than in other parts of the house; it gives the room a secure, cosy feel. The sketches are by Vertès.

BRUCE OLDFIELD

Bruce Oldfield's living arrangements are surprisingly modest, but all the more charming for that. His name is inevitably associated with those of the grand and glamorous ladies he dresses, but if he is a fixture in the social pages of the magazines, and bona fide paparazzi fodder, it is only because he takes his role to heart. He knows better than anyone – and certainly better than anyone based outside Paris or New York – that a couturier has to understand the intimate needs of his clients. Being able to disguise the flamboyant *derrière* and the drooping bosom and, of course, to give every woman a waist is only one aspect of being a couturier. More importantly he must understand about Ascot, debutantes' balls, society weddings, twenty-first birthday parties and the ins and outs of the 'season'. It also translates into creating season-less clothes, because when one's clients flit ceaselessly from Barbados to Cairo to Aspen all in one month, their wardrobe has to be able to cope not only with the changes in temperature, but with the style appropriate to all those society locations.

To understand the lifestyle of the very rich, you have to live it: 'no great hardship', in Oldfield's words. So he can be found dancing with his clients, sharing their agendas, advising their daughters not only on their wedding dresses but on the way to behave whilst wearing them. After almost 20 years in couture, and as its only truly British representative, Oldfield tends to give very good advice, so those jeans-and-sneakers girls who have been dragged along by their elegant mothers often end up developing a couture craving that will prove an expensive addiction for the rest of their lives. British *Vogue* called Oldfield 'a man who charms socially and sartorially'; perhaps the most accurate way of describing the symbiosis of

Opening pages: A comfortable armchair and the fireplace, original to the house, in the top-floor bedroom, and, in the same tones, the exquisite detailing on the collar and button of a jacket. Left: The first-floor living room, purposely dark, and described by Oldfield as moody.

talents that has allowed him to survive the recession-hit 1990s and to emerge at the end of the decade with a brand-new ready-to-wear line and a flourishing client list.

Oldfield, who in 1990 was awarded an OBE, a prestigious British honour, has an unusual background. Parentless, he was brought up by the children's charity Barnardo's in the north of England. He trained as a teacher in Sheffield, then changed direction to study fashion design at Ravensbourne and that cult college, St Martin's School of Art in London. Throughout his career he has devoted himself to charity work in favour of the organization to which he feels he ultimately owes his success, his unofficial role as couturier to the Princess of Wales at the time of her greatest influence enhancing his fund-raising activities. He still has photographs of his Barnardo's foster brothers and sisters in his living room.

Oldfield lives above the shop, an arrangement which has its advantages, because he can just nip downstairs if an important client arrives unexpectedly. The early nineteenth-century building, tall and narrow, with its tiny rooms and awkward staircase, is typical of the terraced rows of Knightsbridge shopping streets. It boasts a first-floor terrace, beautifully planted with gardenias and magnolias in large terracotta pots. Oldfield has transformed the house into the perfect gentleman's quarters, characterized by a subdued manly elegance that is clearly inspired by the art of the 1920s, '30s and '40s which he collects. The living room has putty-coloured walls that gradually darken towards the ceiling, as if due to

Above: A detail of embroidery on an Oldfield dress. Right: On the living room wall, symmetrically placed portraits by Braida Stanley-Creek are flanked by two by Cuthbert Orde. The neutrally grey sofa is furnished with cushions in striped Guillaud fashion fabric.

Above: Oldfield's dressing room doubles as a study: it is here that he keeps his computer, along with regimented rows of polished shoes and neatly hung clothes. The pale wood stool is piled with African cotton sarongs, and the dressing mirror is eighteenth-century French.

'I wanted the decoration to be moody and to suit the actual atmosphere of the house.'

an accumulation of age-old smoke and soot, an effect directly culled from a painting. 'I gave Richard Clarke, the paint specialist, a portrait by Cuthbert Orde from the 1940s for inspiration. It contained all the tones and the mood that I wanted for the room and everything else fell into place. Being a fine artist, he understands what you mean by "something a bit Ben Nicholson".' In the canvases on the walls, in the books on the shelves, in the order and restraint that permeates the atmosphere, in the choice of colours, the influence of Oldfield's legendary fashion elegance is apparent. In his own words: 'It is often quite difficult to know where the apartment ends and work begins. They are inextricably linked in colour, and in a way they work together. My interest in gardening and plants in general, paintings, and collecting fabrics from around the world often shows up in my choice of graphic details in embroidery and prints.'

The house has a theme, much as a collection might. 'I wanted it to be moody and to suit the actual atmosphere of the house as it rises through the floors: as you go higher, the rooms and the staircase feel lighter and airier.' Richard Clarke's paint effect on the staircase, inspired by this idea, is immensely striking: floor by floor, and almost imperceptibly, the colour on the walls moves from chilli red to whipped cream.

Above: The most impressive paint effect in the house, by fine artist Richard Clarke, is on the staircase. It gets progressively lighter in tone storey by storey, changing from glowing red to pale daffodil.

It is a masterful exercise culminating in the cloudy pale blue of the bedroom, perched in the attic, and dominated by a giant bed. The modernity and minimalism of this room is somewhat disorienting after the comfort and richness of the 'womb-like' library, the 'moody' drawing room, even the transitional canary-yellow study-cum-dressing room. Oldfield's friend Mimi O'Connell advised him, saying: 'A bedroom is for fantasy', so he decided to make it 'heaven-like', somewhere he could retire and think.

The kitchen, which opens out onto the luxuriant terrace, is undoubtedly the centre of the house. The walls, like those of the bathroom upstairs, are in raw pink putty, and it is dominated by an extremely businesslike brushed-steel Bulthaup range. 'It not only looks good, but even mediocre cooks like myself can prepare and serve up something edible,' laughs Oldfield. One wonders whether to believe his modesty about his culinary capabilities – the professional battery of pots and pans testifies to his legendary dinner parties. This is also the room where he does his designing: 'I do all my designing at home, surrounded by my personal objects, paintings, plants and colours.' This is an understandable lifestyle decision, given the seductive appeal of the crooked little house, with its early nineteenth-century proportions and its eclectic decoration. 'As a designer, you develop an eye for how things work together. You are not afraid to take risks and you gradually create a style that you feel you can build on and take down different avenues. It is surprising how, in the end, different styles work together. One mustn't be afraid to mix.'

Above: The bathroom, designed with the help of Oldfield's friend Anthony Collet, has pink plaster walls above wood panelling; the engraving is by Terry Wilson. Right: The bed in the ethereally pale blue bedroom was custom-made; the durrie is from Jaipur, and the nude is school of Eric Gill.

OSCAR DE LA RENTA

Despite having left his native Dominican Republic when he was only 17, Oscar de la Renta is undeniably, flamboyantly Latin. He has an exuberance and an exotic accent that betray his childhood on the lush island that he still considers home. He is charming and distinguished, the type of man that Spaniards used to call – in hushed tones of respect – un Señor, a gentleman. He carries himself very straight, yet gracefully, and his conversation is liquid, part-poetry, part-business, spiced up with a generous measure of gossip. He works incredibly hard, and yet never seems to complain nor even to flag, despite being over 60. Fuelled by optimism and certain philanthropic ideals, he moves in the very best of society; indeed, it was at social events organized for the late Duke and Duchess of Windsor that he met both his wives. His late wife Françoise de Langlade was one of France's great women of style, and his second wife Annette Reed is a clever and refined American blue-blood. Having the same social agenda as the distinguished dames who are his clients, de la Renta knows about their love lives and peccadillos, and he understands to perfection their interests and needs.

While de la Renta plainly appreciates and admires women more than anything else, he is himself widely considered one of the most fascinating men in New York. He is a man of multiple talents, and he has devoted only a fraction of them – albeit brilliantly and successfully – to the service of fashion. One of his

Opening pages: A view of the intricately embroidered bodice of an Oscar de la Renta dress opposite one of the cool, dark bedrooms in the Casa de Madera. Left: The veranda. Above left and right: Restful corners and tropical greenery.

friends once insisted in *Vogue* that de la Renta had achieved in 20 years what the Rothschilds had taken two generations to accomplish. In the backbiting fashion industry his name translates as undisputed power and business acumen. A wide range of luxury products bear his logo; the main collection gets shown over a hundred times a season in trunk shows throughout the country; and his three perfumes guarantee his presence in every shopping mall in the land. He seems to represent the attractive world that the consumer at large understandably wants to buy into. He was the first American designer ever to be invited to design a collection for a French couture house – for Balmain in 1993.

Some of his superfluous energy has been channelled philanthropically into the service of various home-grown charities and committees. He is extremely influential in a high-profile but non-political way in his native country – he has been responsible for boosting the country's image by developing an upmarket approach to tourism, as well as providing the impetus for other light industry, and, perhaps most significantly,

Above: The main room in the Casa de Madera: most of the furniture was designed by de la Renta himself and made locally. The experiment provided the impetus for a now flourishing cottage industry.

founding an orphanage and day-care centre that looks after over 600 deprived children. Indeed, he adopted his own son Moses from among the most critical cases. He remains actively committed to the endless fight against poverty still present in the Dominican Republic.

De la Renta's sensitive feel for texture and proportion is equally visible in each of his three homes: 'My favourite way of expressing what I expect both from an interior and from dressing a woman is to use Baudelaire's phrase "luxe, calme et volupté".' In addition to designing fashion, interiors and furniture, the humanist designer is also a talented gardener. It was he who designed the gardens of the magnificent Connecticut home where he spends every possible weekend – 'nesting'.

This house stands in the Casa de Campo enclave that he helped to conceive on an island near Romanes; it was built from scratch, entirely in wood. 'It was inspired by a house in Bangkok that I have always loved, a house built by an American solider called Jim Thompson, who returned to Thailand after

Above: Part of the large collection of blue-and-white china that evokes the Eastern influence behind de la Renta's design for the house. The potted palms and the Moroccan brass pots in the foreground all add to the exotic atmosphere – they are souvenirs of another journey.

the war and became one of the pioneers in the Thai silk business. I have always thought it was wrong to build whitewashed houses in the blinding light and the idea of a structure in lots of different native precious woods, dark and cool, appealed to me: a respite from the sun; something shady and welcoming, where it would be nice to walk around with bare feet.' The house, nicknamed the Casa de Madera, is adjacent to de la Renta's working farm. It has a private beach and self-contained guest bungalows in the grounds. 'Once we get here we never leave the house, it is so pleasant. I have been lucky enough to be married to two ladies who have both had an incredible sense of style; they have made the house fantastically comfortable and cosy ... as if it was created purely for enjoyment. It is the only one of our homes that's like a resort; and as it's right on the water, it's perfect for complete relaxation. I never work here. I can forget all my obligations. I have a lot of childhood friends who live nearby so we just entertain them and have special visitors from Europe and America. I love to have lots of people around – I call it my "little hotel". There's only a problem when it rains: the house is designed for warm weather – but we have masses of beautiful umbrellas!'

Above: The twin-bedded bedroom has a definite colonial feel to it. Again, most of the furniture was made locally and the white cotton drapes and frilled cushions play down the strong lines of the architecture and furniture, giving the room a softer edge.

'What I expect both from an interior and from dressing a woman is … "luxe, calme et volupté".'

De la Renta designed most of the furniture himself, and provided the impetus for a whole new cottage industry when he decided to have it made by local artisans. 'Now they have huge factories,' he laughs, obviously delighted. 'This is my true home: I relate to the exotic. I always wanted a place in the country where I was born. The house has helped me forge a stronger sense of identity, for here I have the impression of still being the same person that left at 17.'

Above left: A dress from the designer's Spring 1997 collection. Above right: A view from the veranda into the bedroom: the house has been designed so that the air can flow freely; wooden slats act as blinds to keep out the heat and brightness of the tropical sun.

YVES SAINT LAURENT

Yves Saint Laurent, probably the most famous fashion designer in the world, has a favourite quote from Proust: 'The magnificent and pitiful family of the hypersensitive is the salt of the earth. It is they, not the others, who have founded religions and produced masterpieces.' Saint Laurent clasps this thought to his bosom as a talisman. The world has always seemed harsh to him: born in the Oman, he was picked on in the classroom, before having to adapt to life in France. Most traumatic by far, however, was when, having been publicly acknowledged as a youthful fashion genius, he was drafted into the Algerian war, for it was then that he had a nervous breakdown. A fragile but brilliant fashion prodigy, he has indeed had to suffer for his brilliance. He is himself acutely conscious of his situation. Writing of his first triumph as heir apparent at the House of Dior, he says, 'At 21 I entered a kind of stronghold of glory that's been the trap of my life.' That day in 1962 there were people in the streets to laud his success, and ever since unmitigated excellence has been expected of him – at the remorseless pace of four collections a year. His fragility has never been kept a secret; rather, it is the prerogative of his aesthetic prowess.

His protective partner Pierre Bergé has wisely created a series of sheltered paradises for him: a Paris apartment stuffed with fine paintings and furniture; a villa in the sumptuous Majorelle Gardens in Marrakech; and a nineteenth-century mansion in Normandy. Without these havens Yves Saint Laurent would have been destroyed by the relentless pressures of the fashion season. Traditionally, he retires to the Château Gabrielle, as the Normandy manor house is known, for August and for the months of May and June: when the banks of purple irises and the hydrangeas flower simultaneously, and early

Opening pages: A heavily embroidered jacket from the Winter 1991–92 haute couture collection and a view of the library, with its nineteenth-century crystal chandelier. Left: Oriental references, such as the bamboo-effect table, abound in the salon. Above right: Verdant growth in the winter garden.

summer brings out the best in this pastoral corner of France, where it rains often and evenings are nicest in front of a roaring fire. Both those periods coincide with designing new collections – 'each time in anguish of not being up to the expectations of the critics, and, more importantly, not being equal to the task itself, not being able to create'.

It was therefore imperative that the house itself be comforting, reassuring, rich with meaning and history. To this end, and in a flight of fantasy, Saint Laurent conceived its decoration entirely around his favourite book: Marcel Proust's *A la recherche du temps perdu* (*Remembrance of Things Past*) – 'the book of my life, I can re-read it ceaselessly. Proust has always been very important to me, very present for me.' The 'autobiographical novel' is incredibly detailed: characters, places, rooms and clothes are described with extraordinary precision, and based on people the novelist knew well, places he had visited, clothes he had seen actually being worn. Proust is certainly unique among his literary colleagues in making fashion such a significant feature in his work; but clothes were to him the reflection of the spirit (or the spirits) of the person wearing them. He was tirelessly meticulous in his efforts to ensure that he made no mistakes; reputedly he used to check with the bartender at the Ritz that what he had written about costume and accessories was completely accurate.

Left: A nineteenth-century armchair in the salon furnished with a delicately embroidered cushion. Above: A *boîte à ouvrage*, or workbox, signed Alphonse Giroux, which was at one time the property of Princess Matilda.

Like Proust, Saint Laurent plays with time. His fashion has, for a long time, been curiously 'dateless' – a concept which might seem far removed from the very essence of the fashion business, hooked as it is on the concept of constant change. Though he is obsessed by collection deadlines, Yves Saint Laurent has ended up going beyond them; somehow the difference between a 1966 Saint Laurent smoking jacket and the 1990s version has become a superficial consideration. Like the rooms and grand balls in Proust, forever stilled, the great French designer has achieved a sense of timelessness in his creations that is usually reserved only for masterpieces of fine art.

Above left and right: Two views of the hall. The mural was inspired by Monet's Nymphéas canvases; the waterlily motif appears throughout the ground floor in different shades: here it is at its lightest. Saint Laurent has also produced several garments that reflect this – his favourite – theme.

There is serendipity in the connection between Proust and Yves Saint Laurent. The writer lived and died in the area, having recorded under the gossamer cape of fiction the lives of his immediate neighbours. Saint Laurent decided to dedicate each of the seven bedrooms of his home to one of these characters: the bedroom called Madame Lemaire, for example, is flooded with roses, because she was a flower painter known, to the witty and waspish set she frequented, as the 'Empress of Roses'. There is a room named after her fictional representation too: Madame Verdurin, she of the relentless soliloquy (often on details of decoration). Saint Laurent's bedroom is named after Swann, the discriminating man about town.

Above: The room named after the Guermantes, a rather unattractive couple who appear in Proust's *A la recherche du temps perdu*. The grandest of the bedrooms, it is meant to recall the atmosphere of the suite that they might have occupied at the Ritz.

The fine paintings and slightly Orientalist atmosphere evoke the fictional hero's more poetic side. Bergé has the dark green and deep purple bedroom named after the Baron de Charlus, a flamboyant, very masculine character. So it continues, room after room. One cannot help but be reminded of the best Saint Laurent couture collections, where *des hommages* to his favourite muses abound: a touch of Callas; the spirit of Chanel; here a wink at Cocteau; here the colours of Matisse, the flowers of Van Gogh; there the drapes of Vionnet. The single-minded homage to Proust here applies the same principle to his house. Both as an exercise in abstract thought and as a decorating experience, it is most exhilarating.

Saint Laurent was aided in his fantasy by Bergé and by their friend, the decorator Jacques Grange. In Bergé's words, 'We didn't have a nineteenth-century decorative scheme in mind. It's not necessarily what we like best, but the house made us do it. It is because we live in this house that we live with this decor. Otherwise we'd have done something else. It was what we call an "*exercise de style*" for the three of us.' Grange adds, 'It is a mad trip around Saint Laurent's references, much like his collections: exuberant, unexpected but controlled. It reflects his approach to fashion much more than any of his other houses.'

Left: Yves Saint Laurent's bedroom, which evokes Proust's central character, Swann. Above: A still-life study in the bedroom, showing a selection of objects that combine to recreate – through their shape, colour and decoration – the essence of the nineteenth century and the *belle époque*.

The idyllic manor, originally built in 1874, is situated in a village a few miles from Deauville, the seaside resort that the Duc de Morny made fashionable. Here, in 1908, the eccentric writer is known to have visited the actress Louisa de Mornand, who was being kept in sumptuous style by a gentleman of means in a house known as the 'Chalet Russe', and it was during that fateful visit that Proust met his editor, Gaston Gallimard, for the first time; the young man had strolled over from his mother's house next door. That significant afternoon in the Chalet Russe seems to have had a particular effect on Saint Laurent, for a few years ago he and Bergé – aided and abetted as ever by Jacques Grange – decided to build a wooden Russian *dacha* in the garden as a kind of cottage, for when they did not want to open up the big house. The view from the lodge is of Russian birch trees, which were specially planted, displaying Saint Laurent's particular penchant for authenticity.

The construction, all of wood, grew out of a visit to Russia in 1986, when a major Yves Saint Laurent retrospective was mounted there. They had been looking to build a garden pavilion for some time, and were keen to incorporate some Moroccan stained-glass panels, but did not want anything too Moorish. The designer had been looking for visual inspiration to no avail, but when they saw the *dacha*, or hunting pavilion, it seemed the perfect solution: the rich colours of the glass would go well, they felt, with wood. Poulayn, the local carpenter, had never had to deal with a commission of this extravagance before, but he made a splendid pine structure, which 'beautifies as it ages' and includes the complex detailing that characterizes the grandest of Russian *dachas*. The interior is charming, particularly because of its

Left: The terrace outside the *dacha,* in the garden of the Château Gabrielle. Inspired by a trip to Russia for an Yves Saint Laurent retrospective in 1986, the 'cottage' was constructed entirely in pine by local craftspeople who had never built anything remotely like it before.

'Proust has always been very

unorthodox combination of influences: on the one hand it is stuffed with authentic Russian artefacts and furniture; on the other, the whole decorative scheme revolves around the huge stained-glass panels that had been in store for ten years, and which Jacques Grange combined with selected pieces of nineteenth-century furniture to produce a rich and luxurious effect. The atmosphere is exotic, and much more successful than if the interior of a real *dacha* had been slavishly copied with stuffy historical accuracy.

Bergé often flies Saint Laurent down to the manor by helicopter, a very twentieth-century way of getting to a retreat that otherwise perfectly recreates a nineteenth-century ambience. This in itself, though,

Above left: One of the eight Moroccan stained-glass windows that Saint Laurent and Bergé had in storage for ten years, before they finally decided to construct this Moroccan–Russian *dacha* around them. **Above centre:** A detail of an outfit in lamé from Saint Laurent's haute-couture collection.

important to me, very present for me.'

is symptomatic of the Yves Saint Laurent fashion attitude: modernity coupled with a perfect understanding of couture. But there is nothing dusty about the Château Gabrielle: the furnishings and textiles may be antique, and the aesthetic turn-of-the-century, but, as Diana Vreeland remarked, Saint Laurent 'lives the way society lives now.' What is more, Grange has done his work with such subtlety and to suit such demanding taste, that there is one major – and happy – difference: it is stuffed with nineteenth-century pieces of a much higher quality than any that might have furnished the villas frequented by Proust. Can Saint Laurent do Proust? The joke, as they say, is on us.

Above left: The main room of Saint Laurent's *dacha*. The jewel-like tones of the stained glass are reflected both in the colourful carpet and the *petit-point* upholstery. Above right: Moroccan mosaic detailing on the fireplace. Following pages: A view of the main room of the *dacha*.

PAUL SMITH

Paul Smith has quietly taken over a considerable slice of the fashion world with his funked-up ready-to-wear lines: bright shirts, a modern interpretation of long, tweed duster coats, fitted 'dandy' suits, tongue-in-cheek T-shirts … the list goes on. What started out as a contemporary take on tailoring has become a worldwide success. In Japan and Paris and in the United States they snap up his work, which explains why, nowadays, he spends such a large proportion of his time – several months of the year – travelling. Smith is a reserved kind of man, true to the stereotype of his native Yorkshire, in northern England; there is no fuss to his conversation, no frills. Yet even he admits to the whole Paul Smith phenomenon being 'very tiring'. His antidote to the stress and weariness induced by transcontinental time-zone travel has proved to be a sprawling Tuscan farmhouse in the wooded hills near Lucca.

The house is ideally situated only an hour away from Florence and Siena, and even closer to the Mediterranean resorts of Viareggio (famously chic in the 1950s with the Vespa boys and girls) and Forte dei Marmi. The latter has more up-to-date big-name boutiques than the average city in Britain or the United States: only in Italy would you find such an obviously fashion-conscious populace indulging in the evening *passeggiata*. Smith, however, is safely hidden away on a plateau between two hills, in the mountains behind Pietrasanta, the town of historic marble quarries, where sculptors from Michelangelo to Botero have lived. Swimming in the calm, calm sea off those well-ordered Italian sands, with their gaily painted

Opening pages: The view over the roof of the house and an ensemble from the Summer 1997 collection. Left: The hand-painted buffet in the hall was found in Paris, the cane chair locally. Above: On display on the buffet, a Tom Dixon candlestick, a Tuscan pottery jug and antique soda bottles.

'The house reflects the clothes I design in

lounge chairs and striped umbrellas, you can see Smith's hills, rising up majestically behind the beach. His neighbours are a different type of Italian, people of the country: farmers and wine growers, and even a *boscaiolo* – a forest warden who tends the thickly wooded hills.

Far from Forte dei Marmi's cosmopolitan atmosphere, Smith lives a very 'country' existence. 'We live well away from everybody, and are extremely antisocial,' admits Smith, 'but that is why we bought such an isolated house. All our neighbours are locals: we didn't buy a house in Tuscany to spend all our time with the ex-pats.' Smith bought the house in the mid-1980s with his painter girlfriend Pauline Denyer-

Above: The living room, with a comfortable, traditional English armchair upholstered in Manuel Canovas fabric. Books and small ornaments are stored in a painted cupboard fronted in chicken wire which was bought in a Paris flea market. The painting is part of a series of wartime canvases.

the importance of colour and simplicity.'

Smith, an ex-Slade student. They had just sold a house in England and, over a dinner in Paris, they impulsively decided to re-invest the money in property straight away, rather than frittering it on furniture or paintings. They had some close friends who suggested Tuscany, and though they hardly knew the area, they caught a plane to Pisa and started looking. They visited ruin after ruin and finally settled on the most derelict, a farmhouse that had not been lived in for more than 20 years. Although the area is clearly Mediterranean, there is a greenness about it that is reminiscent of the lushness of certain areas of the English shires – pre-Industrial Revolution, and with double the sunshine.

Above left: A decorative iron armillary sphere, a present to Paul Smith from his girlfriend, stands in the fireplace, which is not often used because Smith usually only spends the summers in the house. Above right: A suit from the 1997 Paul Smith collection.

'We loved the fact that it was not a villa but a farmhouse, and that we would be surrounded only by Italians who had lived there all their lives. The peace and the privacy is what attracted us the most. That and the thousands of trees.' In line with their search for authenticity, the couple spent two years quietly restoring their find with the help and advice of the local *geometra*. They flew out from England to supervise the work, staying at the Principessa Hotel in Lucca and combing the countryside to source old tiles and replacement beams, so that the house could be restored with only period materials. The whole process

took longer than had originally been expected, so there was time to scour the local antique shops and markets for simple, rural furnishings – with rich results. They also shopped for furniture in London and at their favourite Paul Bert flea market in Paris.

Architecturally, their main concern was to open up the house to the light, 'so that the terrace could become the main living room, and we could bring the outside in'. They pierced the façade with three large arches and built a terrace which, complete with a marble-topped table, is their favourite corner. 'We spend most of the time outside as we are mainly here during the summer. Surrounded by the countryside, the people and the fantastic food, every moment is enjoyable.' The couple did all the decorating themselves: 'As the farmhouse was derelict when we chanced upon it, we wanted to

Above: The hand-painted wardrobe in the master bedroom, which came from an antique shop in Lucca. The walls have been painted with water-based paint in the original colours: blue and green, with a dark red dividing line.

Left: This bedroom is situated at the top of the house and has a high, beamed ceiling. The bedside tables were acquired locally, but the chest of drawers was brought over from England.

Above: A detail of the delicately painted panel on the wardrobe which stands as the central piece in the sparsely furnished and summery master bedroom.

recreate the feel of when it was first built. There were still traces of the original colours on the walls, so we had them re-mixed in a very transparent water-based paint, which doesn't penetrate the wall evenly, and gives a very interesting effect, which we like to think is probably quite close to the original.' From tiny fragments of paint and plaster, they managed to establish that some of the rooms had been bi-coloured, the two tones separated by a thin, rusty red line. Now they have a green and pale blue bedroom, a blue dining room, and a yellow and green entrance hall, as well as a traditional ochre façade.

This interest in colour is reflected in Smith's fashion work: when he first burst on to the scene, his brightly coloured men's fashions represented a revolution for the then dull palette of men's clothes. 'The house reflects the clothes I design in the importance of colour and simplicity. Being a designer has made me more conscious of the visual aspects of the interior: such things as proportion.'

Early on during the building Smith made the decision not to use the house as an escape for the weekends but instead only to spend long periods there at a time – a month or more. 'It always takes me about a week to calm down and relax anyway. That's when I begin to enjoy it; I do a lot of mountain biking in the hills. I like the idea of living here and not just passing through: when you stay for a month you really begin to feel as if you belong.'

Above: A view of the entrance hall, looking through to the dining room. **Above right:** Despite their different origins, the Italian table and French chairs in the dining room sit happily together. Manuel Canovas fabric was used to cover the cushions. The painting dates from the 1940s.

Left: Wooden chairs and a marble-topped table on the terrace; most meals are eaten here during the summer.

Above: Local produce is often brought over by the neighbours, who cultivate vines and grow vegetables – zucchini so fresh that they still bear their flowers, just right to cook as a regional delicacy.

VALENTINO

Jackie O, Babe Paley, Gloria Guinness, Jacqueline de Ribes, Marella Agnelli ... a list that catalogues the uniquely elegant women of the twentieth century would differ little from Valentino's client list, past and present. He arrived in Paris to begin the fashion training that he had precociously decided upon for himself in 1950, when Dior's postwar extravagance of line was at its peak. The sublime glamour of that time has been religiously preserved by the then absolute beginner: Valentino is today the world's grandest designer. He supervises 24 collections a year from his palatial headquarters in Rome's historical Piazza Mignanelli and, in a rather neat turnabout of conventional expectations, he has a lifestyle beyond that of many of his clients' wildest dreams. His office looks more like that of an eighteenth-century grandee than that of a designer, but then, with the sort of turnover that his company commands, fashion becomes an economic force to be reckoned with. As he tends to remind interviewers, when they become caught up with such frivolities as why Sharon Stone agrees to catwalk for him, it is 'a *serious* business'.

He owns six houses: his main home on the Via Appia in Rome, a chalet in Gstaad, a Peter Marino-designed Fifth Avenue apartment, a villa on Capri and a recently acquired château near Paris, as well as the five-storey Knightsbridge town house featured here. He also owns a celebrated 140ft yacht, fitted out entirely in blue and white, for which the description 'floating palace' could have been invented. Valentino has an extraordinary gift for decoration and he pays great attention to order and to detail. He becomes passionately interested in such questions as fabrics, trimmings or finishes. He intervenes in a very personal way, despite the pressures of his fashion empire-building: 'While we were finishing the house I flew in to

Opening pages: One of a pair of bronze hunting dogs on the living-room mantelpiece, opposite a detail of a dress from the 1990–1 couture collection.
Left: Antique silver boxes and part of the designer's collection of Meissen porcelain on an eighteenth-century mahogany table in Valentino's bedroom.

London every weekend to check the state of it, and then back to Rome for my work. I lived a commuter's life for six months!' The same scented atmosphere of contained calm and faultless housekeeping permeates all his homes: lighting is always controlled and adjusted in order 'to make women feel beautiful when they come and visit'. Much like his couture clients, his homes are *soigné*, as the French put it: well kept. There are many anecdotes that circulate about Valentino's fastidious attention to detail in this respect; and it has been verified that the linen curtain around his oversized mahogany bed and the linen skirt of his bath are carefully pressed twice a day when Valentino is 'in residence' in London. In the

gracious Victorian stucco-fronted house, amid the white half-moon of one of Knightsbridge's most elegant terraces, Valentino's arrival must have reintroduced standards not seen since the last days of the Empire.

Since his Lombardian childhood, when he demanded made-to-measure suits from his parents, Valentino has never been attracted to the charms of the fashionable distressed look and when he decided to decorate his new acquisition in the pure English style, it was a foregone conclusion that he was not

Above left: One of Valentino's many monkey statuettes. Above right: A view of the front drawing room with its Aubusson carpet. The checked silk used for the curtains here is the same fabric that is used to line the walls in the back drawing room.

referring to 'shabby chic'. Essentially, a Valentino house must be, above all, a setting fit for women dressed in the clothes he designs. Re-live, in your mind's eye, the ballroom scene from Luchino Visconti's *The Leopard*, one of Valentino's favourite films: any one of his interiors has to be up to performing as a foil for one of those sumptuous women. 'Usually I don't change the basis of my essential style in my houses. Style in fashion changes all the time; you should be more faithful in decoration.'

Above: An arch acts as the division between the front and back drawing rooms. Despite their divergent decorative schemes, identical eighteenth-century marble fireplaces and a consistent use of the same checked fabric lend a sense of unity to the space as a whole.

Valentino acquired his London house in order to spend more time in one of his favourite cities. 'When I visit it is purely a social trip, and relaxing. I love it here and gather a lot of inspiration by going to the theatre and seeing my friends who live here. It's also nice to have a house and not an apartment. I love the layout of those town houses: no big spaces, but lots of charm.' The interior was 'not bad, but full of flowered chintz, and as a man I could not live with that. I worked with Tom Parr of Colefax & Fowler, although the work was mainly undertaken by Roger Banks-Pye.' Banks-Pye, who died a few years after completing the house, had brought a highly individual approach to Colefax & Fowler, the decorating company that is the most romantic bastion of Englishness. He was to prove the perfect accomplice for Valentino's determined line on the traditional interior, as he was not opposed to turning tradition on its head, and Valentino would insist on such revolutionary proposals as using frock fabric for walls and curtains, and oversized furniture for every room. 'Being a fashion designer definitely affects the approach one has to the decoration of a house ... they would make their proposals but I knew exactly what I was looking for. I needed someone who perfectly understood my ideas and aims and could interpret them.'

Left: The eighteenth-century English mahogany four-poster bed with Italian embroidered sheets which date from the nineteenth century. The bed curtains, which are in toile à beurre, are pressed twice a day. The sofa is upholstered in blue silk. Above: The bath, with its linen bath surround.

'Style in fashion changes all the time; you should be more faithful in decoration.'

Valentino's forceful approach imposed itself swiftly; he was looking for something more aggressive than conventional English style. Happily, Roger Banks-Pye's credo – 'Always scale up, not down. Everyone is terrified of making things too big. If in doubt, make it larger not smaller' – suited the designer perfectly. They installed 'important' pieces of furniture that sometimes appear to be almost as big as the rooms: the master bedroom's four-poster is a case in point. Together they discarded the traditional wisdom about contrasting patterns and colours not being used in small spaces, and they turned Valentino's London address into a sumptuous residence, quite unlike anything Colefax & Fowler had ever produced before.

Valentino was satisfied. 'I have never been a "minimalist". All my homes are full of objects and furniture which I have collected on my travels. I love going to antique shops all over the world. My London home was the fifth residence that I had decorated and by then I had collected an array of furniture and objects which I moved there. I love checked fabric; all my homes feature a variety of checks in different colours. In fact, they all have a great mix of fabrics and even the smallest details are accurately dealt with – as in my fashion work.'

Only one Valentino detail is missing: his pugs. They usually follow him everywhere. 'The quarantine laws ...' he arches his eyebrows and turns down his mouth in distaste. As if to compensate, the house has a theme, as a fashion collection might: animals. They are everywhere, from the Meissen 'substitute' pugs to monkeys in the pattern of the toile de Jouy fabric on the walls. As you walk through the house, on every floor and in every room, there are objects that portray the theme: dogs, monkeys, panthers and many more. The accumulation enables Valentino to refer to his luxurious house as 'The London Zoo'.

Above: A detail of the sumptuously sequinned back of a couture jacket. Right: Toile de Jouy lines the walls in this guest bedroom. A 1799 architectural engraving by Audebert hangs above the bed; in an alcove beside it stands a nineteenth-century Russian bookcase.

GIANNI VERSACE

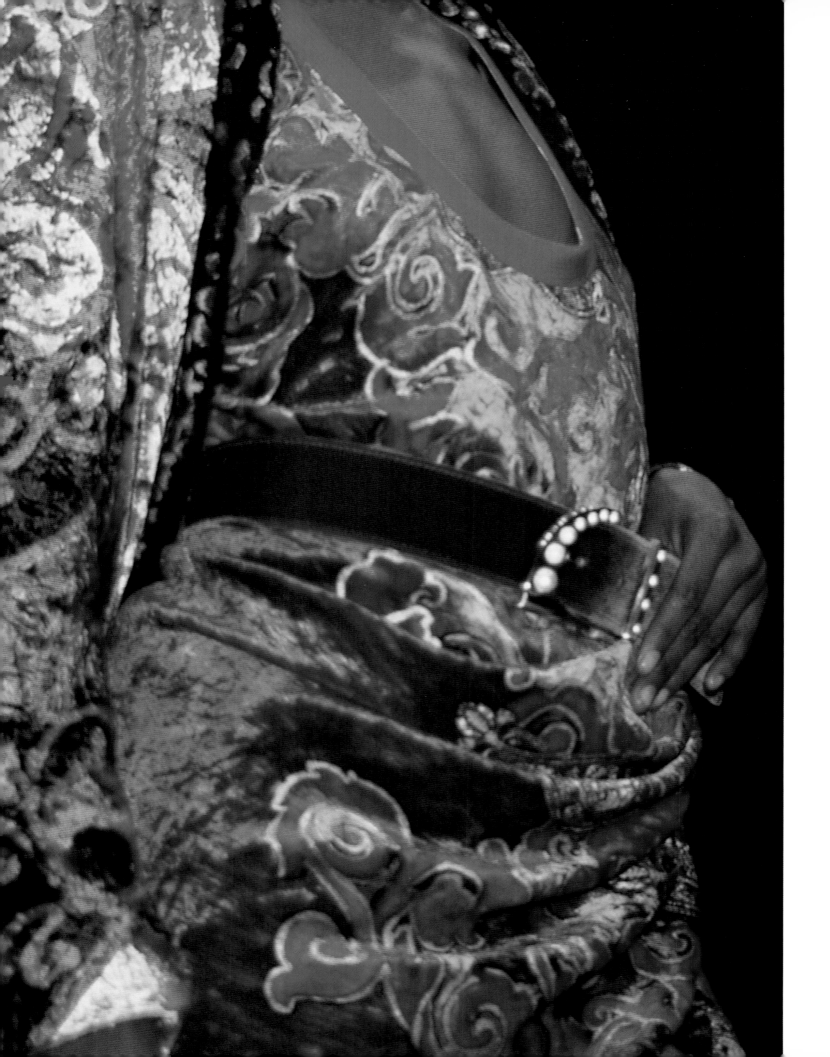

When Gianni Versace discovered Miami's flamboyant South Beach, it was love at first sight. For the designer who once famously retorted 'I don't care about good taste or bad taste, I just care about fun', Miami had everything. It was funky, modern, happening and hot – just like he was. On his first visit he was supposed to be en route to a holiday in Cuba. 'I stopped in Miami for a day to attend the opening of a Versace boutique. Since I only had a few hours to visit the city, I asked for a good driver who could show me the real Miami, where I could find colour, atmosphere and the beautiful people. He took me to the News Café on South Beach where I started feeling emotions that reminded me immediately of Capri and Saint-Tropez in their golden years. Although it was different, certain things about the atmosphere reminded me of the sense of fantasy and creativity that I had felt in those years: an incredible sense of freedom. I had not felt those emotions for a long time. I changed my plans, cancelled my trip to Cuba and decided to stay in Miami. There was something in the air that I found incredibly attractive. I spent the afternoon driving round different parts of town. I went to Key Biscane, where the landscape became wilder; I went from Bal Harbour to Coconut Grove, and finally I went to visit the magical Palace of Vizcaya. I was in love with Miami and when I eventually left for Italy, all I could think about was returning to Florida. The second time I visited Miami, I had already decided I wanted to have a house there.'

Miami, from its 1970s image as a pensioners' haven, had indeed changed beyond recognition. For one reason or another, and quite unexpectedly, certain parts of the planet become fashionable, desirable and cool almost overnight. Post-*Miami Vice*, South Beach suddenly boasted a new café society of sun-

Opening pages: A detail of Fontana Decorazioni's painting on the drawing-room ceiling and two neo-classical Empire armchairs upholstered in Versace fabric. Left: A close-up of a Versace Atelier dress, with the same richness of pattern and texture as Versace's pleasure palace.

kissed youth: surfers, models, starlets, architects, artists and photographers. Its invariably sumptuous climate made it the perfect photo-shoot location, and the beach was something akin to the world's largest open-air studio. The buzz had already attracted such glitterati as Ron Wood, Sylvester Stallone, Mickey Rourke and Madonna, all of whom had houses there.

When, 'in love with the atmosphere', Versace bought a crumbling pleasure pile in 1992, he knew that his neighbours would be part of that rock 'n' roll crowd that he both dresses and hangs out with. Casa Casuarina, named in 1930 after a Somerset Maugham book of short stories (set in a suitably decadent colonial Borneo), had an intriguing history. Architecturally, depending on your point of view, it could either be classified as a pastiche mishmash or as an important slice of South Beach cultural history. When Versace bought the pile, saving it from being transformed into a shopping mall, the original 24 apartments and owner's penthouse had become fairly seedy, bohemian, rented accommodation.

Versace, who is by definition a connoisseur of the art of high pastiche, embarked on a lavish restoration, winning over even the most adamant preservationists. 'Quality is the most important thing for me,' he has often said, imposing the highest standards on finishes, whether in the atelier or on the building site. Reverentially, he sent teams to hunt high and low for original roof tiles and fittings; he commissioned murals, frescoes and painted ceilings; and had mosaics laid in the pattern of Versace scarves. The decorating job turned into a total rebuild, in part because he flamboyantly decided to acquire the neighbouring Revere Hotel as well, in order to raze it and give himself a garden and swimming pool.

Above: A fine *lit-bateau* 'dressed' in Versace fabric. Right: An ornate balustrade around a light well in a hallway, illuminated by an original stained-glass skylight. Following pages: The wood-panelled sitting room with its specially made velvet upholstery. The pictures are both by Picasso.

'I don't care about good taste or bad taste, I just care about fun.'

To give the project manager, landscape designer and architect an idea of both Versace's decorative preferences and the standards they were expected to work to, they were dispatched to Europe. Versace arranged for them to tour Versailles and the grandest Venetian palaces as well as his palazzo in Milan and his wondrously restored eighteenth-century villa on Lake Como. Casa Casuarina absorbed all these influences in its two-year renovation to become grander and more splendid than it had ever been.

Versace was personally involved in every decorating decision: 'I like to choose all the furniture and decorative objects for my house, including tablecloths, china and glass. I bought all the furniture from antique dealers around the world: Rome, Paris, London and New York. Being a designer means being an aesthete, being a creative person. It is unthinkable that I should give free range to an interior decorator when one of my houses is involved. A decorator is, of course, very helpful, but I feel that my houses

Above: Two views of the pebble-mosaic grotto which acts as the Versace family dining room. It was painstakingly decorated by Fantini Mosaici, a traditional Italian firm. The theatrical appearance of the room is in keeping with the original owner's fantasy of an extravagant Miami retreat.

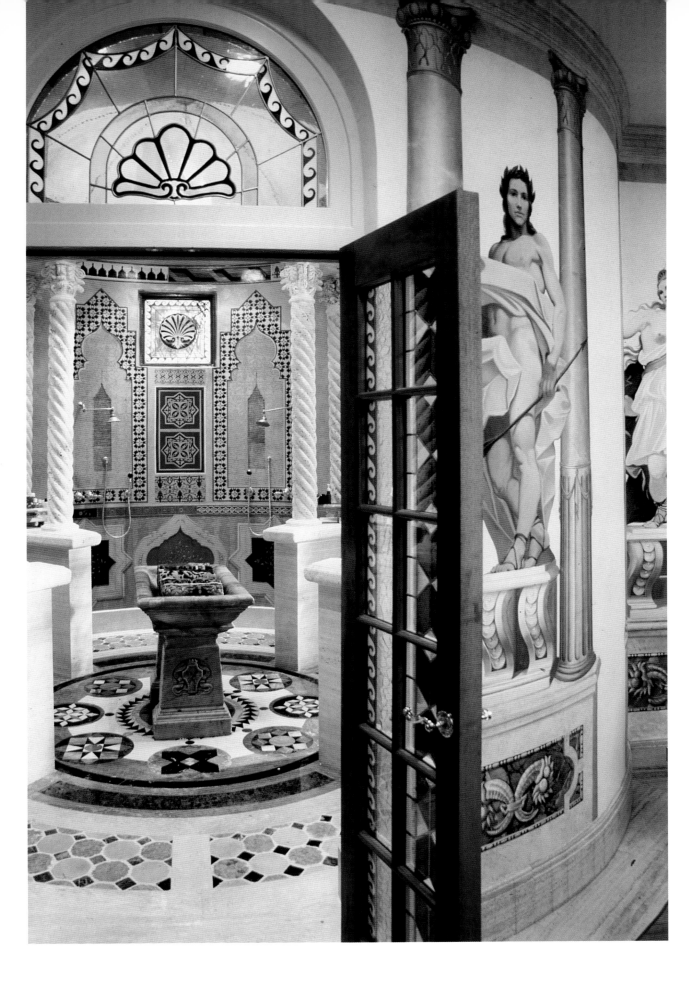

Left: The shower room, designed along the lines of a Moorish *hammam*.

are part of me and part of my life. I have a real passion for interiors. I started to design my Home Collection because of my love for houses, and some of the prints I originally designed for my shirts and scarves have now either become part of that line or part of my own home.'

The extravagant mansion was to inspire his catwalk collection the following season – sketched in the heady euphoria of the lavish restoration. And non-stop, nubile Miami continues to be a constant influence throughout his work. 'It has a unique energy. When I restored the house I tried to evoke the atmosphere of vitality, freedom and creativity that I felt the first time I came to Miami because that's what made it "love at first sight". I like to come here directly after the shows to get some rest. It can be very private and incredibly silent. But there is always the opportunity to have guests over and organize parties. Miami is very vibrant, a lot of my friends have houses here.

'Sometimes I spend a holiday just relaxing, but I also work very well here: the light and the colours are very inspiring. I generally design at home. Days in the office fly by – with my assistants and meetings, fittings – whereas I often find the time and power of concentration to work on new ideas at home. The studio has a beautiful view of the ocean and working here is really special.'

The original owners, a well-heeled homosexual couple, whose taste embraced a cosmopolitan range of styles, would have been thrilled to know the well-dressed re-incarnation of their creation. They had faithfully tried to recreate the house of Columbus's son in Santo Domingo, but Versace felt 'that the location allowed for crazy colours and the mixing of different styles'. His references range from neo-classical to Pompeian with a touch of Moorish fantasy, an extravagant mix of cross-cultural decorative touches: stained glass, mahogany panelling, marble and gold bathrooms, wrought iron. His Medusa's head motif is incorporated into everything: from mosaics, to tableware, to specially woven velvet upholstery. 'I love to be surrounded by beautiful things and of course I have my style.'

Left: The central courtyard, inspired by early American neo-colonial architecture, has a strong Moorish feel. The busts are original to the house.
Above: The swimming pool, built on the site where the Revere Hotel once stood. The mosaics were inspired by one of the designer's prints.

INDEX

AUTHOR'S ACKNOWLEDGMENTS

THIS BOOK WOULD NOT HAVE BEEN POSSIBLE WITHOUT MY WONDERFUL assistant Anna Davenport, who brought organization and optimism to the project.

Thank you to Sophie Djerlal for picking up the pieces, my agent Maggie Philips for her unflagging support and to my editor Denny Hemming for entrusting me with the project. Alison Martin allowed me to write under her roof and Gillian Baoughey was there for me as usual.

At the offices of the various designers credit must go to: Maximiliano Modesti and Farida Khelfa at Azzedine Alaia; Dominique de Roche, Clara Saint and Danielle Leclerq at YSL; Isabella Capecce at Armani in Paris; Russell J Nardoza at Geoffrey Beene; Roberta and Antonio at Romeo Gigli; Margaret van Buskirk at Isaac Mizrahi; Catherine Klein at Michel Klein; Anna Gardner and Karen Milne at Joseph; Carlos Souza at Valentino; Anna Maria Stradella and Tidi Minqueti at Gianni Versace; Susan Seelback at Oscar de la Renta and my dear Nancy at Nicole Farhi.

Erica Lennard, who has proved herself a kind friend, was on hand for our photographic emergencies, as was dear Roland Beaufre. Dominique Dupuich most kindly stepped in to style the Koji story at short notice.

Last but not least, I would like to extend a particular thanks to Eric Bergère who looked after me far beyond the call of duty. Pierre Bergé of YSL was very helpful and encouraging.

PUBLISHER'S ACKNOWLEDGMENTS

CONRAN OCTOPUS WOULD LIKE TO THANK the following photographers and organisations for their kind permission to reproduce the photographs in this book:

1 Jean Pierre Godeaut; 4–5 Erica Lennard/Conran Octopus; 8 Niall McInerney; 9 © Prosper Assouline; 10–13 Erica Lennard/Conran Octopus 13 right courtesy of Azzedine Alaia; 14 left courtesy of Azzedine Alaia; 14–15 Erica Lennard/Conran Octopus; 16 courtesy of Azzedine Alaia; 17 Erica Lennard/Conran Octopus; 18–19 Santi Caleca; 20–1 Nicolas Millet(stylist: Gilles Dalliere)/ Agence Top; 22–3 Nicolas Millet/Marco Polo; 24–25 Nicolas Millet(stylist: Gilles Dalliere)/ Agence Top; 26 left Santi Caleca; 26 right Andreas Them/Camera Press; 27 Santi Caleca; 28–35 Oberto Gili/Courtesy House and Garden © 1989 The Condé Nast Publications Ltd; 36 left Michel Arnaud; 36–7 Oberto Gili/Courtesy House and Garden © 1989 The Condé Nast Publications Ltd; 38–47 Roland Beaufre/Conran Octopus; 48 Piero Biasion; 49 Fritz von der Schulenburg/The Interior Archive; 56 Simon Brown/Conran Octopus;

57–62 left Oberto Gili/The Condé Nast Publications Ltd/British Vogue; 62 right Anthea Simms; 63 Oberto Gili/The Condé Nast Publications Ltd/British Vogue; 64 Michel Arnaud; 65–72 left Santi Caleca; 72 right Andrew Lamb/The Condé Nast Publications Ltd/British Vogue; 73–5 Santi Caleca; 76–82 Martyn Thompson courtesy of Elle Decoration UK; 83–4 Simon Brown/Conran Octopus; 85 Martyn Thompson courtesy of Elle Decoration UK; 86 Christoph Kicherer (Yves Marbrier); 87 Chris Moore; 88–9 Christoph Kicherer (Yves Marbrier); 90 left Eric Morin; 90–3 Christoph Kicherer (Yves Marbrier); 94 left Christoph Kicherer (Yves Marbrier); 94 right Eric Morin; 95 Christoph Kicherer (Yves Marbrier); 96 Guy Marineau/Java Fashion Press Agency; 97–103 Erica Lennard/Conran Octopus; 104–7 Roland Beaufre/Conran Octopus; 108 left Anthea Simms; 108–9 Roland Beaufre/Conran Octopus; 110 left Roland Beaufre/Conran Octopus; 110 centre Anthea Simms; 110 right Roland Beaufre/Conran Octopus; 111–13 right Roland Beaufre/Conran Octopus;

114 Tim Griffiths; 115–16 Henry Bourne/Elle Decoration; 117 Ray Main; 118 Henry Bourne/Elle Decoration; 119 left Andrew Lamb/The Condé Nast Publications Ltd/British Vogue; 119 right Ray Main; 120–1 Henry Bourne/Elle Decoration; 122–23 Horst Thanhäuser/Picture Press; 124 left Missoni Press Office; 124 right Roland Beaufre/Agence Top; 125 Roland Beaufre/Agence Top; 126–8 Horst Thanhäuser/Picture Press; 129 Roland Beaufre /Agence Top; 130 Nikki Taylor/Rex Features; 131–5 Pascal Chevalier/ Agence Top; 136 Anthea Simms; 137–8 Pascal Chevalier/Agence Top; 139 left Michel Arnaud; 139 right Pascal Chevalier/Agence Top; 140 James Mortimer/World of Interiors; 141 Simon Brown/ Conran Octopus; 142 James Mortimer/World of Interiors; 144 left Simon Brown/Conran Octopus; 144–5 Simon Wheeler; 146–9 James Mortimer/World of Interiors; 150 Anthea Simms; 151–6 Jacques Dirand/The Interior Archive; 157 left Anthea Simms; 157 right Jacques Dirand/The Interior Archive; 158 Piero Biasion; 159–70 Marianne Haas; 170 centre Piero Biasion;

170–3 Marianne Haas; 174 James Mortimer/The Interior Archive; 175 Chris Moore/Paul Smith Ltd; 176–7 James Mortimer/The Interior Archive; 178–9 Jean Pierre Godeaut; 179 right Chris Moore/Paul Smith Ltd; 180 left James Mortimer/The Interior Archive; 180–3 Jean Pierre Godeaut; 184 Fritz von der Schulenburg/The Interior Archive; 185 Piero Biasion; 186–191 Fritz von der Schulenburg/The Interior Archive; 192 Piero Biasion; 193 Fritz von der Schulenburg/ The Interior Archive; 194 Tim Street Porter/Elizabeth Whiting & Associates; 195 Michel Arnaud/Jahres Zeiten Verlag Syndication; 196 Anthea Simms; 198–9 Michel Arnaud/Jahres Zeiten Verlag Syndication; 200–1 Tim Street Porter/Elizabeth Whiting & Associates; 202–5 right Michel Arnaud/Jahres Zeiten Verlag Syndication; 207 Anthea Simms; 208 Eric Morin

Every effort has been made to trace the copyright holders. We apologise in advance for any unintentional omission, and would be pleased to insert the appropriate acknowledgment in any subsequent edition.